MYTHOLOGY AND CULTURE WORLDWIDE

Chinese Mythology

MICHAEL V. USCHAN

LUCENT BOOKS
A part of Gale, Cengage Learning

GALE
CENGAGE Learning·

Farmington Hills, Mich • San Francisco • New York • Waterville, Maine
Meriden, Conn • Mason, Ohio • Chicago

© 2014 Gale, Cengage Learning

WCN:01-100-101

LIBRARY OF CONGRESS CATALOGING-IN-PUBLICATION DATA

Uschan, Michael V., 1948-
  Chinese mythology / by Michael V. Uschan.
    pages cm -- (Mythology and culture worldwide)
 Summary: "The Mythology and Culture Worldwide series from Lucent Books is designed to help young readers understand the origins, cultural importance and impact of world mythologies. Each volume focuses on one cultural or national mythology. Major myths, characters, gods and goddesses, and themes of the mythology are presented with a particular emphasis on tying these stories back to the geography, history, natural resources, technological state, social organization, religious beliefs, and values of the culture that created the mythology"-- Provided by publisher.
 Includes bibliographical references and index.
 ISBN 978-1-4205-1146-8 (hardback)
 1. Mythology, Chinese--Juvenile literature. I. Title.
 BL1825.U74 2014
 299.5'1113--dc23
                                                    2014002516

Lucent Books
27500 Drake Rd.
Farmington Hills, MI 48331

ISBN-13: 978-1-4205-1146-8
ISBN-10: 1-4205-1146-7

Printed in the United States of America
1 2 3 4 5 6 7 18 17 16 15 14

TABLE OF CONTENTS

Map of China

Major Characters in Chinese Mythology

Character Name	Pronunciation	Description
Ao Bing	ow-bing	God of rain
Bashe	bah-shih	Giant mythical snake
Cai Shen	tsai-shen	God of wealth
Chang'e	chong-ihr	Goddess of the moon
Confucius		Wise sage
Dragons		Mythical creatures that fly
Eight Immortals		Eight humans who became divine
Fu Xi	foo-shi	Brother of Nu Kua
Guandi	gwan-dee	God of war
Guanyin	guan-yin	Goddess of mercy
Jade Emperor		Powerful god in heaven
Jiangshi	jyong-shee	Vampire or zombie
Jingwei	jing-way	Mythological heroine
Laozi	lau-dsee	Founder of Daoism
Lei Gong	lay-gong	God of thunder
Mazu	mah-tsoo	Goddess of the sea
Monkey King		A monkey that became a god
Nu Kua	new-kwah	A goddess that created humans
Pangu	pahn-goo	A giant that created the world
Shangdi	shong-dee	The supreme god in heaven
Shen-nong	shen-nawng	God of farming
Siddhartha Gautama	si-DAR-ta GAW-ta-ma	Founder of Buddhism
Sui Ren	sway-rehn	God of fire
tian	tee-ahn	Heaven
Xi Wangmu, Queen Mother of the West	shi-wong-moo	The most powerful female goddess
Yan Wang	yahn-wong	King of hell
Zao Jun	dzau-jhong	God of the kitchen

A Confusing Galaxy of Ancient Myths

Chinese mythology encompasses an extremely large collection of fantastic characters and amazing and bizarre legends, tall tales, and stories. As a result, it is perhaps the most complex and difficult mythology of any nation or culture to understand. Yuan K'o is a college professor from the People's Republic of China and a mythologist, an expert on mythology. He has devoted his life to researching his country's vast, intriguing mythology. He says, "There is in fact a treasure trove of ancient Chinese myths, and they are so extraordinary, so magnificent, and so full of imaginative power that they stir the human soul to its very depths."[1]

The divine beings and fantastic characters and animals that inhabit Chinese mythology include Nu Kua, a goddess credited with creating the first human beings; she had the body of a serpent and the head of a beautiful woman. Other beings include hungry ghosts, which are the spirits of dead people. They harm the living if the living do not offer them ceremonial food and money during an annual festival known as Ghost Day.

The dragon is the most popular fictional creature in Chinese mythology and is featured in many myths. There are also strange creatures, such as the qilin, which has the head of a dragon and the body of a tiger, and the Bashe, a snake so big it feasts on elephants. Another odd creature in Chinese mythology is the jiangshi, which is variously described in literature as a vampire or zombie that moves by hopping and kills people to absorb their qi (chi), the life force important in Chinese medicine and martial arts.

Despite the exotic lure of the many fantastic elements that make it so bizarre and entertaining, Chinese mythology is not as well known as mythologies from other countries and cultures. This is partly because Chinese mythology, unlike mythologies that originated in Greece, Italy, and Scandinavia, has no central cast of characters or main family of deities. Instead, the mythological beings and different types of stories are so vast and complex that Chinese mythology can confuse people when they first encounter it. But despite its highly exotic nature and lack of uniformity, Chinese mythology has served the same psychological and cultural purposes for the Chinese as mythologies of other countries have for their people.

Mythology Explains the World

Myths are stories about supernatural beings, ancestors, or heroes that attempt to explain a natural phenomenon, a belief, or a practice, and a mythology is the collection of myths of a particular people. Early civilizations did not have the means to record their myths, so people shared them with each other and with their children orally, by relating the myths out loud. This preserved the myths until later generations learned how to write. These myths, passed from parent to child for generations, were vitally important in shaping a people's history and culture. According to mythologist Kenneth C. Davis, people began creating myths to explain things they did not understand. He explains,

> It is the object of the myth, as of science, to explain the world, to make its phenomena intelligible. [Myth] really answers a fundamental need of the human mind. [Myths] came into being because people couldn't provide scientific explanations for the world around [them]. Natural events, as well as human behavior, all came to be understood through tales of gods, goddesses, and heroes.[2]

In early Chinese mythology, a giant named Pangu raised the sky above the Earth, and when he died, his body parts were transformed into the sun, moon, and other parts of the natural world.

Primitive people were awed and mystified by the natural world in which they lived. The changing state of weather, especially when it turned violent, amazed and frightened them, because they had no scientific explanations for such powerful natural phenomena. To make sense of what had frightened and awed them, they made up stories about why such things happened. Chinese mythology says that various gods in heaven control various aspects of weather. For example, Lei Gong, whose name in English is Duke of Thunder, is the god who makes the loud, frightening noise that sometimes accompanies rain.

In addition to myths about the weather, ancient Chinese people made up stories about how the world was created. For example, they did not understand why the sky, sun, moon, and clouds were so high above them. They explained it in the myth of a giant named Pangu, who had horns on his head and who grew 10 feet (3m) per day for eighteen thousand years. It was his astonishing height that made it possible for him to raise the sky far above the earth. When Pangu died after his prodigious feat, his body parts were transformed into the sun, moon, and other parts of the natural world.

The same human need to explain natural phenomena was also used to explain abnormal human behavior, such as a murderous rage that transformed a normally gentle person into a killer. As a result, primitive people created myths that blamed gods or evil spirits for making people behave wickedly. It was these myths that helped to instill moral behavior and create deeply ingrained social attitudes in various cultures. In his book *Chinese History: A Manual*, mythologist Endymion Porter Wilkinson claims the results of these myths can be found today in cultures around the world. He writes, "Myths are the basis for understanding of any society [because] they reveal the values and beliefs not only of the earliest people who lived in that society, but also of later generations who codified and passed down the elaborate mythology that generations of children learned from their mothers and [other elders]."[3]

Although some myths are based on negative human traits, other myths perpetuate the good in people. One example of this type of myth is the Chinese story of Jingwei, an emperor's daughter who drowned in the East Sea. She came back to life as a small bird that dropped stones and small twigs into the sea to fill it up so it could not kill anyone else. Jingwei thus became a symbol to Chinese people of the perseverance and determination they needed to finish any task they attempted, no matter how impossible it seemed.

Such myths are also important because they explain human nature, which has not really changed since the myths were created thousands of years ago. Mythologist J.F. Bierlien believes that those myths are not only a portal to the past but also a reflection of attitudes, feelings, and beliefs that human beings retain today. In his book *Parallel Myths*, he writes, "Myth is an eternal mirror in which we see ourselves. Myth has something to say to everyone, as it has something to say about everyone: it is everywhere and we only need to recognize it."[4]

CHAPTER 1

China

Chinese mythology has one of the most interesting and imaginative stories of how human beings were created. After the world was formed, the goddess Nu Kua wandered through it. She admired the mountains, rivers, oceans, and trees and was happy with the animals and other creatures that she encountered. But when Nu Kua became lonely, she decided to make people. This is how one ancient Chinese text claims she did that: "Nu Kua kneaded yellow earth and fashioned human beings. Though she worked feverishly, she did not have enough strength to finish her task, so she drew a cord through the mud and lifted it out to make human beings. That is why [royalty] are the human beings made from yellow earth, while ordinary poor commoners are the human beings made from the cord [being pulled through the mud]."[5]

Nu Kua is one of the most well-known characters in Chinese mythology. There are, however, many different versions of the myths about her. Because of the many different Chinese dialects, her name may appear as Nuwa Nu Wa, Nugua, or Nu Gua. Most artistic representations of Nu Kua show her with the head of a woman and the body of a snake, but some renderings give the goddess a human head and a body of a dragon, sometimes with dragon claws extending from her torso. In most of the Chinese myths, Nu Kua is female, but in some of the earliest tales about her, it is impossible to tell her gender. Another puzzling discrepancy concerns Nu Kua's relationship with the male god Fu Xi. In some myths Fu Xi is her brother, and in others he is her husband; some myths even claim Fu Xi helped her create human beings.

The many variations in Nu Kua myths, from how she looks to what her name is, cast doubt about which versions are correct and illustrate why people have difficulty studying

Most artistic representations of Nu Kua show her with the head of a woman and the body of a snake or dragon.

Confusion over Written Chinese

One of the difficulties in studying anything about China is the way in which Chinese names and words are translated into English. In the late nineteenth century, people from Western nations began using the Wade-Giles system to transcribe Mandarin, China's official language, into words spelled with letters of the Western alphabet. Then in 1979 the People's Republic of China created the pinyin system for transliteration, because they believed it was a more accurate way for Westerners to write spoken Mandarin. The problem is that the switch to pinyin resulted in new spellings for many Chinese words. Thus, Communist leader Mao Tse-tung became Mao Zedong, and China's capital city, which had been known for centuries as Peking, became Beijing. This has resulted in a body of material that has been transliterated using two different systems: the older Wade-Giles system and the newer pinyin system.

Chinese mythology. Similar factual differences also exist about other characters and stories from Chinese mythology. This lack of consistency is due to China's vast size, huge population, numerous languages, and variety of cultures, factors that have also influenced the history and cultural growth of China itself.

An Ancient Civilization

China is the world's third-largest country in size after Russia and Canada. Its landmass encompasses 3.74 million square miles (9.69 million sq. km), making it slightly larger than the United States, which is 3.71 million square miles (9.61 million sq. km). China has an estimated population of 1.3 billion people, more than any other nation, and that population includes fifty-six different ethnic groups. However, the vast majority of China's people (91.5 percent) are Han, people descended from the Han dynasty that ruled China from 206 B.C. to A.D. 220.

Since 1949, when Communists won political control of this ancient nation, China has been known as the People's Republic of China (PRC). But for thousands of years before that, ruling power was passed down through descendants of a single family. Over time, the succession of rulers from the same family was considered a dynasty. The myth in which Nu Kua creates humans played an important cultural role in the acceptance common people had in being ruled by royal families. The Nu Kua myth was considered proof that members of royal families were superior and had a divine right to rule because Nu Kua had taken more time and effort to create people considered royalty than she did common people.

China has one of the world's oldest continuous civilizations, one that began in 2100 B.C. with the founding of the Xia dynasty. However, people had been living within China's present-day borders much earlier than that. In the early twentieth century, archaeologists discovered fossils of primitive ancestors of human beings near Beijing, China's capital. The finding proves that humans dwelt there 750,000 years ago. Other archaeological evidence shows that China's earliest human settlements date to about 5000 B.C.

The Xia, the first Chinese dynasty, was established in prehistoric times, the period in any society before people learned to read and write. The Xia dynasty is believed to have existed from 2970 B.C. until 1600 when the Shang dynasty came into power and became the first dynasty to leave written records of its history.

Early Dynasties

The Shang dynasty, which ruled the Yellow River area of China from 1600 B.C. until 1046 B.C., is notable for many technological advancements that changed Chinese culture and the way people lived. In addition to introducing written records, the Shang dynasty improved methods of producing bronze, a metal composed of copper and tin, and invented the horse-drawn chariot for warfare. The Shang, however, never ruled all of China. For more than a thousand years, China was divided into separate states, ruled by competing dynasties that often fought each other for control of territory.

Qin ruler Zhao Zheng was the first emperor of China and established the Qin dynasty.

It was not until 221 B.C. that the Qin dynasty defeated the armies of six other states—the Han, Zhao, Yan, Wei, Chu, and Qi—to unite most of the area that makes up present-day China. Led by Zhao Zheng, the first emperor of all of China, the Qin dynasty only lasted until 206 B.C., when the Han dynasty used military force to defeat the Qin and assume control of China. Despite the Qin dynasty's brief control over all of China, it is the Qin name that led to present-day China's name. When English and French historians transliterated the Chinese characters for *Qin* into the Western alphabet as *Ch'in*, they gave the nation its Westernized name of China.

The Han dynasty extended China's influence into Korea and other parts of Asia and was responsible for important technical advancements, including inventing paper and the seismograph, which can detect earthquakes. During this period, the first Chinese dictionary appeared, and Sima Qian wrote *Shiji* (*Records of the Grand Historian of China*), the first comprehensive history of China. Sima, a second-century historian employed by the Han emperor, used written records to write his book. China was one of the first nations to create a written form of communication, an important milestone in its cultural development.

The First Emperor, Zhao Zheng

Zhao Zheng of the Qin dynasty was the first emperor of a united China. He was known by the name Shi Huangdi, which means "first emperor." Zhao ruled China from 221 B.C. to 210 B.C., after his Qin dynasty conquered rival dynasties to win control of China.

Chinese Writing

Archaeologists have found samples of Chinese writing dating back to 1200 B.C. The earliest writing discovered is on oracle bones, which are pieces of turtle shell or animal bone on which people carved questions they wanted the gods they worshipped to answer. A shaman—a person who was believed to have mystical powers to foretell the future and perform magic—would then apply a heated metal rod to the bones until they cracked. The shaman would then interpret the pattern of cracks to answer the question. This was one of many techniques of divination, a method by which people try to communicate with divine beings to answer questions or to see into the future.

Chinese writing differs from writing in Western nations. Instead of using separate letters, such as *A* or *B*, to spell words, the Chinese use a system of characters, each of which represents a single syllable of spoken Chinese. The Chinese began using these characters to write messages by inscribing them on a variety of surfaces, the first of which were bones and rock. The various materials available to write on, however, were not ideal, and China became one of the first civilizations to invent paper.

In his book *Science and Civilisation in China*, Tsien Tsuen-Hsuin credits a man named Cai Lun with learning how to produce paper. He writes, "In ancient times writings and inscriptions were generally made on tablets of bamboo or on pieces of silk [but] silk being costly and bamboo heavy, they were not convenient to use. [Cai Lun] then initiated the idea of making paper from the bark of trees, remnants of hemp, rags of cloth, and fishing nets."[6] Although primitive types of paper had existed in China since the second century B.C., Cai Lun is credited with inventing paper in A.D. 105, because his manufacturing process vastly improved its quality.

Inventing a form of writing and creating paper, which could easily preserve and transmit this new form of communication, changed life in China as much as the development of the Internet did for the world in modern times. People were able to write messages that allowed them, for the first time, to communicate easily with other people, even those who lived thousands of miles away. In addition, writing and paper enabled people to document history and what their lives were like for future generations. Until these developments, any accounts of history, culture, or mythology could only be transmitted orally, and their validity was suspect because no one knew whether they were altered as they were passed down from generation to generation.

Written records left no doubts about what people were trying to explain or what they believed when they wrote them. However, some early historians included information in their writings about prehistoric figures, events, and customs from oral traditions that were only myths. And it is this mix of fact and fiction in China's early histories that help make Chinese mythology so confusing and hard to understand.

A Fragmented Mythology

The first authors who researched Chinese myths combined bits and pieces of mythology from written inscriptions on rock, metal, and other objects that had survived for centuries, as well as from oral stories that had been told for an even longer period of time. It was like trying to piece together a jigsaw puzzle. In his book *Larousse World Mythology*, French historian Pierre Grimal, an expert on world mythologies, writes, "The important thing is [that] what one understands [as] 'Chinese mythology' can only be [viewed as] a relative-

The Importance of Mythology

In his book, Don't Know Much About Mythology: Everything You Need to Know About the Greatest Stories in Human History but Never Learned, *Kenneth C. Davis explains that mythology is still important today. He writes,*

As old as humanity, the first myths belong to a time when the world was full of danger, mystery, and wonder. In the earliest of human times, every society developed its own myths, which eventually played an important part in the society's daily life and religious rituals.

One of the chief reasons that myths came into being was because people couldn't provide scientific explanations for the world around [them]. Natural events, as well as human behavior, all came to be understood through tales of gods, goddesses, and heroes. These same ancients "invented" the myths that grew hand in hand with their civilizations, making it impossible to separate one from the other. [These] ancient legends are still a powerful force in our lives today. They remain alive in our art, literature, language, theater, dreams, psychology, religions, and history.

Kenneth C. Davis. *Don't Know Much About Mythology: Everything You Need to Know About the Greatest Stories in Human History but Never Learned.* New York: HarperCollins, 2005, p. 10.

ly complete, comparatively well-interpreted collection of a mass of fragments of varied origin."[7]

One reason there are so many different versions of myths about characters such as Nu Kua is that China was not united when many of the tales were first created. Mythologies from Greece and Scandinavia are consistent because the people who made them lived in a unified nation and shared a common culture. But Chinese mythology evolved from the myths of millions of people living in separate states that often warred against each other and that had different cultures. According to Lihui Yang, a professor of folklore and mythology at the College of Chinese Language and Literature at Beijing Normal

The Chinese Calendar

China is believed to have the world's oldest calendar. The Chinese began using it during the third millennium B.C. and still consult it for ceremonial occasions. Chinese mythology says the inventor was the mythical Huangdi, the Yellow Emperor, who reigned from 2698 B.C. to 2599 B.C.

University, the cultural differences of the people creating the myths further fragmented Chinese mythology. In her book *Handbook of Chinese Mythology*, cowritten with Deming An, she writes, "Since almost every ethnic group has its own mythical gods and stories [there] is not a systematic, integrated, and homogenous 'Chinese mythology' held and transmitted by all the Chinese people. Even among Han people [the vast majority of Chinese], there is not an integrated system of myths."[8]

A second factor that damaged the uniformity of oral myths about important characters like Nu Kua was that the people who created them spoke many different languages. Inaccurate translations in ancient times undoubtedly created errors and discrepancies in myths, when people who spoke different languages exchanged them.

The third reason there are so many variations in Chinese mythology is that China had no main religion that bound its people together. Instead, Chinese mythology descended from four different religions, all of which contributed different gods, goddesses, and other characters and stories to the grand universe of Chinese mythology.

Folk Religion

The simplest and earliest Chinese religion was folk religion, which developed during the Shang dynasty. Central to this primitive religion was animism, a belief that natural objects, such as mountains, hills, rivers, trees, rain, and even thunder and lightning, possess divine spirits. In Chinese religion this belief is referred to as *shen*, which means "gods" or "spirits." The Chinese believed that if they prayed and made sacrifices to them, *shen* would grant these worshippers what they wanted. For example, farmers prayed to *shen* that controlled rain to end droughts and to *shen* of the soil in which they grew crops to give them a bountiful harvest. An ancient history book explains how Emperor Shun, a mythical figure from China's prehistory, made such sacrifices for the well-being of his people: "When he sacrificed to the hills and rivers, he did so to the spirits supposed to preside over the hills and rivers of note in all the kingdom, and thereby exercised his royal prerogative, for in subsequent ages each feudal lord sacrificed to the hills and rivers in his [kingdom]."[9]

Shang practices that became part of folk religion included human sacrifice. When rulers died, scores of people were killed and buried with them, so their spirits would accompany the ruler into the afterlife. A similar rite involving human sacrifice was common in other primitive cultures, including that of Egypt. In his book *Chinese Mythology*, mythologist Anthony Christie describes the remains of such victims that have been discovered in Shang dynasty tombs. He writes, "Sometimes the human victims had been beheaded and their heads placed in separate heaps from their bodies. These may have been prisoners captured in battle. All these victims seem to have died to furnish the dead lord with 'servants' in the next world."[10]

A concept of heaven also developed during the Shang dynasty. Instead of being the place where souls of good people traveled after they died, as in Christianity, the Chinese heaven, known as *tian*, is simply home to a wide variety of divine beings. In that respect it is similar to Asgard, the home of Norse gods, such as Odin and Thor. And unlike Christians, Jews, and Muslims, the Chinese did not believe in one omnipotent god. They prayed and made sacrifices to hundreds of deities, including the kitchen god Zao Jun, who people believed protected their homes and families.

During the Shang dynasty, ancestor worship also became ingrained in Chinese society. People believed that if male members of their family prayed to and offered sacrifices to their ancestors, the spirits of the dead would help them. The offerings included food, animals, and paper that mimicked money and was burned so their ancestors would be rich.

In his book *Don't Know Much About Mythology*, Kenneth C. Davis explains why ancestor worship became important to Chinese families. He writes, "With proper sacrifice, the eternal soul became a deity of power and influence that could respond to [prayer] requests or perform other

Ancient Chinese folk religion had many gods and spirits, called shen. *Pictured here is Zao Jun, the kitchen god.*

heavenly favors [for its descendants]. If a deceased ancestor's soul was neglected or treated poorly, that soul could become a demon and haunt the living."[11] The myth that dead ancestors could wield power to help the living was key in creating family pride and respect for the dead, an integral part of Chinese culture.

Folk religion was a primitive religion that is most closely associated with China's rural population, the vast majority of which was poor and illiterate. Eventually three other religions evolved in China that the royalty and the upper class favored over folk religion. They were known as "the three teachings"—Confucianism, Daoism, and Buddhism.

Philosophical Religions

Confucianism and Daoism began in China about twenty-five hundred years ago, while Buddhism came to China from India in the first century A.D. These newer religions focused on philosophies that instructed people how to live better lives instead of merely believing in spirits and deities. They

Myths and Chinese Scholars

Yuan K'o, a college professor in the People's Republic of China, has devoted his life to studying Chinese mythology. According to him, one reason China's mythology is not as well-known as those of other nations is because ancient scholars failed to seriously study and write about it. Yuan says that many upper-class Chinese who wrote histories, dramas, and other books looked on myths with ridicule, because the people who cherished them were poor and uneducated. He believes some scholars valued mythology so lightly that they intentionally left some mythic tales out of the books they wrote, which meant that they were lost for all time. According to Yuan, this scholarly neglect is one reason Chinese mythology is not as complete as those of other nations. He explains,

Finally and most important, Chinese myths were prevented from becoming fully developed by the negative attitude of scholars of the early Chinese empire and throughout the centuries [who] viewed the fantastic elements and anti-social aspects in tales of marvels and wonders with a very deep prejudice, ignoring their imaginative flair, color, emotive power, and deeper levels of meaning. As a consequence, they did not consider it important to preserve myths in written records, and so in time Chinese myths were neglected and many lost forever.

Yuan K'o. Foreword to *Chinese Mythology: An Introduction* by Anne Birrell. Baltimore: Johns Hopkins University Press, 1993, pp. xi-xii.

also taught people codes of morality and ethics that helped them lead good lives.

Daoism (more commonly spelled as Taoism/Tao) was founded by Laozi (more often spelled as Lao-tzu), a sixth-century-B.C. philosopher. The religion takes its name from the Chinese word *Dao*, which means "way" or "path." Daoism claims people can live happily, if they live a virtuous life, meaning they are not selfish or do not seek to destroy the balance of nature. Although Daoism incorporates many folk religion myths, it also created new ones about heaven as well as its own populous pantheon of gods, spirits, and mythical animals. Daoism also invented mystical beliefs, including the theory that people can live forever if they meditate and exercise properly.

Confucianism is named after Kong Fuzi, a philosopher who lived in the fifth century B.C. and is known in the West as Confucius. Confucianism is an ethical and philosophical system that incorporates ancestor worship and stresses respect for family. It also advocates living a moral life by following the Confucian version of the Golden Rule, which advises individuals to treat other people as they would want to be treated by others.

Buddhism was transplanted from India and is based on the teaching of Siddhartha Gautama, known as the Buddha, who lived in the fifth century B.C. Buddhists believe people struggle all their lives against the impulse to always seek pleasure instead of trying to help others. Buddhism is based on a belief that life in this world is suffering. It offers a way of release from that suffering through meditation, moral living, and right beliefs, which were taught by the Buddha. Over the centuries, many myths and folk beliefs have been incorporated into Buddhism.

Confucianism, Daoism, and Buddhism had a greater impact on Chinese people than did folk religion, because these philosophies gave people moral guidelines on how to live. Confucianism, for example, outlines proper relationships people should have with family members and government officials. Daoism explains how people can live in harmony with nature and other people and how to improve their physical health. Buddhism teaches people they can be happy if they are content with what they have and do not desire things they do not have.

Kong Fuzi, known in the West as Confucius, taught that Confucianism is an ethical and philosophical system that incorporates ancestor worship and stresses respect for family.

However, the Chinese never viewed their religions the way Christians, Jews, and Muslims did. Instead of going to temples or churches on certain days to pray, make sacrifices, and worship various gods, the Chinese often performed those religious functions before altars in their homes. When Chinese people did go to religious temples, the structures often housed images of divine beings from several different faiths, because most Chinese adopted practices and beliefs from several religions.

Hampden C. DuBose, a Christian missionary in China during the late nineteenth century, was amazed that the four religions coexisted so peacefully. In his book *The Dragon, Image, and Demon*, DuBose writes, "China is the only country in the world where [multiple] systems could stand side-by-side without one expelling or superseding the other."[12]

An Isolated Nation

The Han dynasty ended in A.D. 220 and was followed by a period of disunity and instability that lasted more than three centuries. The Sui dynasty unified China again in A.D. 589, and various dynasties then ruled the huge, populous nation for most of the next fifteen hundred years. The last to rule China was the Qing dynasty, which was in power from 1644 to 1912, when Puyi stepped down as the last emperor.

One of China's greatest accomplishments was building the Great Wall, the largest human-made structure on earth.

During its long history, China dominated other Asian countries not only because of its size but also because of its scientific advancements. The Chinese are best known for inventing paper, gunpowder, the compass, and printing. Other Chinese innovations include kites, the water wheel to harness energy, the seismograph to record earthquakes, and the decimal system. One of China's greatest accomplishments is the Great Wall of China, the largest man-made structure on earth. Constructed over centuries in northern China to keep out invaders, the wall is 13,171 miles (21,197km) long. Its length includes 3,889 miles (6,259km) of tall, fortress-like walls as well as trenches and natural defensive barriers, such as hills and rivers.

Later the Great Wall became a symbol of the isolation China imposed on itself in modern times. In 1793 when British king George II sent gifts to Qianlong of the Qing dynasty, the Chinese emperor rejected them by saying, "There is nothing we lack. We have never set much store on strange or [foreign] objects, nor do we need any more of your country's [manufactured goods]."[13]

The emperor's brash attitude reflected the Chinese belief that they were superior to outsiders and better off not having any contact with the rest of the world. By the end of the nineteenth century, China's self-imposed isolation had weakened the nation by cutting it off from scientific and educational advancements in other parts of the world. This isolation resulted in a poorly functioning nation. During this period, the Chinese people also lost faith in their ability to rule because Western nations and Japan had begun to dominate them politically and economically. On January 1, 1912, Puyi was forced out of power, ending nearly two thousand years of dynastic rule.

Civil War

The civilian and military leaders who assumed control of China after Emperor Puyi left in 1912 renamed the country the Republic of China, a name associated with democracy instead of royal rule. The new government wanted to strengthen China by educating its mostly illiterate population, establishing a democracy, and modernizing the nation with technological advances, such as electricity, that were largely absent from the country. The Guomindang (Chinese Nationalist Party) used superior military and political power to win control of most of China. But the Guomindang then struggled to govern the new republic, because warlords, military leaders with large armies, still controlled parts of the country. The Guomindang also was unable to win popular support when it failed to improve the lives of the vast majority of Chinese who continued to live in dire poverty. When the Chinese Communist Party (CCP) was founded in 1921, it began a civil war against the Guomindang for the right to rule China.

The civil war between the Communists and the Guomindang continued until the Communists claimed victory on October 1, 1949, and established the People's Republic of China. The Communists tried to ban religion and force people to quit believing in Chinese myths. However, most Chinese refused to give up the religions and myths they had always known. Belief in tales about Chinese deities, worship practices, and Chinese religion survived attempts by Communists to purge them from Chinese society, and they are still alive in the twenty-first century.

CHAPTER 2

Creation, Mythical Beasts, and Evil Spirits

C hinese mythology contains some of the most inventive stories and strange characters that exist in any of the world's mythologies. The fantastic quality of Chinese mythology is easily seen in tales of how the world was created and the mythical beasts and evil spirits that are believed to inhabit it. These myths include the tale that parts of the physical world were formed from a giant broken egg and that a giant that emerged from that egg created people. Other Chinese myths populated the world with dragons that could fly and the spirits of dead people and demons that wanted to do harm. Despite the exotic, almost whimsical nature of these unusual tales, the ancient Chinese created them for an important purpose. Such myths were attempts to explain how and why things happened.

Perhaps the most important myths in any culture are creation myths, because the primary mysteries ancient people everywhere puzzled over was how their world had been created and where they themselves had come from. Many creation myths are connected to various religions and are recounted in texts that are considered sacred. Judaism and Christianity are two examples, and these two religions even share the same creation story: God created the world and all living things in six days and then rested on the seventh day.

Although many cultures have one main creation story, the Chinese have several different stories. However, according to mythologist Anthony Christie, the conflicting creation accounts in Chinese mythology all serve a similar purpose. In his book *Chinese Mythology*, he writes, "Philosophically, for the Chinese as for other people, creation was the act of reducing chaos to order, a theme which persists throughout Chinese thought [and mythology]."[14]

Chaos into Order

The various Chinese creation myths all say that before creation the only thing that existed was an elemental unknown nothingness that had no tangible shape, form, or human life. According to the *Huainanzi* (The masters/philosophers of Huainan), which was written in the second century B.C., "Before heaven and earth had taken form all was vague and amorphous. Therefore it was called the Great Beginning."[15] Another ancient book describes what existed before the world was created. It reads, "Heaven was formless, an utter chaos; the whole mass was nothing but confusion."[16]

Chinese creation stories as well as those in Greek, Egyptian, Mesopotamian, and Babylonian mythologies all use the term *chaos*, which refers to an unformed void that existed before creation. The Chinese word for this is *hundun*, which means "primordial chaos." The need to bring order out of chaos is evident in how people worshipped Shangdi, one of the earliest Chinese gods.

As late as 1538, a prayer that Ming dynasty emperors offered to Shangdi credited the god with creating the world and the human beings that populated it. According to Hampden C. DuBose in his book *The Dragon, Image, and Demon*, "Of old, in the beginning, there was the great chaos without form and dark [and] neither form nor sound. Thou, O spiritual Sovereign, camest forth and first didst divide the grosser parts from the purer. Thou madest heaven, Thou madest earth, Thou madest man. All things got their being [from you] with their reproducing power."[17]

This particular myth is the only one that says one divine being created the world and human life. There are, however, several Chinese myths that claim to be the true story

One of the earliest Chinese gods was Shangdi, who is credited with creating the world and human beings.

of the creation of the world and its inhabitants. All of them are attempts to bring order to stories about how the world came to be. The Chinese desire for order is also reflected throughout Chinese philosophy. This was especially true in how they thought they should be governed. Throughout several thousand years of rule by emperors, Chinese people accepted the right of royal families to govern them because it fit the order of life they believed in. And philosophers, such as Confucius, stressed orderly relationships between family members as the key to a happy life.

The Cosmic Egg

China is one of several cultures, including India and Finland, with creation accounts that are considered cosmic-egg myths, because they involve an egg that gives birth to the

Pangu

Works of art featuring the giant Pangu vary greatly in how they depict him. Some art shows Pangu with long hair covering his body and two stubby horns on his head. In others Pangu is bald and more human looking. However, Pangu is almost always shown holding up the sky.

world. Although bird eggs were part of the diet of primitive people, they surely must have been mystified when baby birds emerged from eggs they normally ate. The miraculous transformation that occurred inside an egg probably inspired primitive people to believe their world could have been created in the same way.

The Chinese version of this cosmic-egg myth centers on Pangu, who, according to an ancient written account, was born in an egg and began the creation of the world by breaking out of it. According to the account, "In the beginning there was darkness everywhere, and Chaos ruled. Within the darkness there formed an egg, and inside the egg the giant Pangu came into being. For eons, safely inside the egg, Pangu slept and grew. When he had grown to gigantic size, he stretched his huge limbs and in so doing broke the egg."[18]

The egg broke into two pieces; one half of the eggshell became the earth and the other half became the sky. Pangu, who was already a giant when he emerged from the egg, continued to grow at a rate of 10 feet (3m) per day for eighteen thousand years until he was 30,000 miles (48,280km) tall. The myth explains that Pangu had to keep growing, because he needed to separate the earth from heaven. The immense effort of separating the earth and heaven, which primitive people believed existed above the sky, exhausted Pangu so much that he died after completing his task.

The second part of the Pangu creation myth is as fantastic as the first. It states that after Pangu dies, his decomposing body makes the various elements of the physical world. According to an ancient Chinese text:

When [Pangu was] approaching death, his body was transformed. His breath became the wind and clouds; his voice became peals of thunder. His left eye became the sun; his right eye became the moon. [His] flesh became fields and land. His head and beard became the stars; his bodily hair became plants and trees. His teeth and bones became metal and rock [and his] sweat and bodily fluids became streaming rain.[19]

The myth also states that small bugs on Pangu's body became the first Chinese people. However, another myth about the creation of human beings states that Nu Kua, the goddess with the head of a woman and the body of a snake, created people. One myth from Daoism explains how the concept of yin and yang, which is central to Daoist philosophy, emerged from chaos when the world was created. The yin-yang concept states that the world is divided by polar-opposite energies or qualities such as dark and light and male and female and that people need to learn to live with both to have peaceful lives.

When Pangu emerged from the cosmic egg, he kept growing to an enormous height in order to separate the earth from heaven.

Gifts from the Gods

Even though humans were responsible for such important innovations as writing, the Chinese came to believe that they were gifts handed down from divine beings. In her book *Chinese Myths*, Anne Birrell explains how those myths evolved:

> China has numerous myths of the origins of culture and human society. These [myths] contain the statement that a certain deity 'was the first' to grant a gift of culture, or that a deity 'taught humans how to use' the divine gift. [The myths] emphasize that it was the deities who invented and discovered cultural benefits rather than humans, and this conveys the idea of divine control over human life.[20]

In one myth, Sui Ren, whose name means "fire driller," is the god who teaches humans how to use fire. He comes from a faraway land where Sui trees grow. These trees have branches that easily produce fire when rubbed together. When Sui Ren came to China, he taught people how to make fire. He took a small stick, stuck one pointed end in wood shavings that had been placed atop another stick, and then began rotating the stick swiftly between his hands. The technique gave Sui Ren his name because it looked like he was trying to use one stick to drill through the second. In reality the drilling action produced enough heat to ignite the shavings and start a fire.

Many other cultures have similar tales that describe friendly gods that introduced fire to their ancestors, because fire was vitally important to primitive people. For example, in Greek mythology the god Prometheus gave people the gift of fire. Fire made it easier for primitive people to live and survive, because it provided light and warmth, as well as a way to cook food and scare away dangerous animals. Like other peoples, the Chinese honored and revered their fire god for teaching them how to make fire by praying to him and giving thanks to him with offerings of food.

There are several other myths about how people learned to make fire. One says that Huangdi, a mythical ancient leader known as the Yellow Emperor, taught people to make fire by rubbing sticks together instead of using the drilling technique. Both primitive methods, however, can create fire. Huangdi is also said to have taught people to cook food

The Silk Empress

The Chinese were the first to discover how to weave silk from the cocoons of silkworms. It is believed the Chinese have been spinning silk from this substance since 3750 B.C., because silk cocoons were discovered by archaeologists in a site dating back to this ancient period. Chinese mythology credits Leizu, the wife of Huangdi, with discovering how to produce silk from this insect substance. Her feat won her the title of the Silk Empress. Before silk, people wore clothes made from animal skin that were uncomfortable. According to the Handbook of Chinese Mythology, *written by Lihui Yang, this is how Leizu discovered silk cocoons in mulberry trees and learned to weave silk:*

She found some cocoons [and] silk threads that came out of those cocoons were so light, soft, and tough!

Leizu was excited when she realized that she could make cloth from the silk. She then picked many cocoons and took them back home. She ordered women to reel the silk from the cocoons. [Then] Leizu began to weave. At first, she tried to imitate the spider's weaving but failed, because the silk was not as sticky as the spider's thread. One day when she went out to fish, she saw a big fish swimming back and forth freely between the reeds. She then thought that she could weave by using a shuttle shaped like a fish to weave back and forth between the silk threads. Her method proved effective. She quickly wove a piece of fabric and formally named it "silk." She then taught all the women of her clan the skill of weaving.

Lihui Yang. *Handbook of Chinese Mythology.* Santa Barbara, CA: ABC-CLIO, 2005, p. 166.

This lithograph shows silk production in China. Chinese mythology credits Huangdi's wife, Leizu, with the discovery of silk.

instead of always eating it raw, which made it taste better and killed bacteria that could make people sick.

Shennong is the god of agriculture, and he also helps people avoid sickness from food. Chinese mythology says this god took pity on people because he saw they were making themselves sick and dying from eating and drinking poisonous plants. Shennong taught people which plants were safe to eat as well as how to plant wheat and other crops. He also invented the plow and is often depicted pushing one. Some artistic renderings of Shennong show him with the head of an ox, the animal that usually pulled plows in China. Myths also say that this god used his knowledge of plant life to teach people how to use plants as medicine to heal themselves when they became sick.

Another myth about who taught people how to plow and plant crops says the god Hou Qi invented the plow and showed people how to plant various types of grain. And there is a very unusual story, even for Chinese mythology, about how people learned to plant and eat rice, which has always been the most important food in their diet. It involves not a god but a dog. The myth says that after a devastating flood, "a dog was seen to emerge from a waterlogged field. From its tail there hung bunches of yellow ears full of seeds, which people planted in the wet, but drained fields. The seeds grew and the plants ripened to give the people rice."[21]

The gratitude the Chinese had for the dog for introducing them to rice led to a tradition of giving cooked rice to dogs after the vital grain was harvested.

Chinese Dragons

While many myths feature animals that are real, some myths are about mythical creatures. And no mythical creature is more important in Chinese mythology than the dragon. In 1984 archaeologists unearthed a jade figure of a coiled dragon that had been buried with a man in Liaoning Province. The tiny dragon, which is only 4 inches (10cm) tall, is the earliest known depiction of China's most honored and celebrated mythical creature. Chinese dragons are far different from those in Western mythology and fictional works, such as *The Hobbit*, written by J.R.R. Tolkien. Smaug, the dragon in *The Hobbit*, conforms to the Western image of a dragon—a massive, evil creature that flaps giant wings to fly and emits jets of fire. But Chinese dragons can be any size, even as small as a caterpillar. They are generally good instead of bad and do not have wings, even though they can fly. And they do not breathe fire. DuBose writes, "The fabulous dragon of China [has] no wings, and when he rises in the air, it is by a power he is supposed to possess of transforming himself at pleasure. He can make himself large or little, and rise or fall, just as he chooses. The dragon [has] a prominent place in Chinese mythology; he sends rain and floods, and is the ruler of the clouds."[22]

Artworks depicting dragons usually show them with slim, snake-like bodies and short arms with curved claws. The brightly colored dragons, which are usually yellow and red, are covered with scales and have bony ridges along their backs. Their heads, which are topped by horns, have elongated jaws like a crocodile with impressively large, sharp teeth and snake-like tongues. Images of dragons often show them with a pearl attached to their mouths or lodged under their chins. The pearls contain magic and are the dragon's most prized possession.

Dragons became revered mythological creatures because they have magical powers to control rainfall and water in lakes and streams. The ancient Chinese even believed that every body of water had its own dragon, which lived in a palace beneath the water's surface where it kept gold, jewels, and other treasure. In times of drought people prayed to dragons for rain. Zhou Chongfa, an archaeologist from Hubei Province in China, believes primitive people invented dragons because they wanted to believe in a source of divine help that they could call on to help them. He explains, "As farming and animal husbandry began to take the place of hunting and fishing [as] the main source of food, human beings prayed for good weather for crops, and the imaginative figure of dragon has been gradually created as an agriculture numen [spiritual force]."[23]

The Jian

One of the strangest creatures in Chinese mythology is the jian, a bird that has only one eye and one wing. Two of these strange birds had to work together so they could fly. The name of this fictional bird became a nickname for couples that are deeply in love.

Chinese Dragons

The dragon is a mythical animal that is deeply rooted in Chinese culture. It has been revered by the Chinese and closely associated with its rulers for centuries. Everyone from average people to the emperor revered dragons and often worshipped them. The Chinese loved and respected dragons so much that they adopted this mythical creature as a symbol of their nation. The website ChinaCulture .org explains the deep emotional bond the Chinese have always had with dragons:

[In] China, the dragon is credited with having great powers that allowed it to make rain and control floods by striking the river with its mighty tail, for example. Dragons are also revered for their ability to transport humans to the celestial realms after death. They are symbols of the natural world, adaptability and transformation. . . . In the minds of the early Chinese people, the dragon was a god that embodied the will and ideals of the Chinese people.

ChinaCulture.org. "The Almighty Dragon." www .chinaculture.org/gb/en_chinaway/2004-02/25/con tent_45896.htm.

The Chinese people loved and respected dragons so much that they adopted the mythical creature as a symbol of their nation.

Most Chinese dragons are beneficial. In the tale "Three Sovereigns and Five Emperors" Yinglong, a rare winged dragon, helps the equally mythical Huangdi defeat Chiyou in a battle for control of China. Some dragons, however, cause problems. For example, the ancient Chinese believed dragons were responsible for lunar eclipses. Today people know that the moon orbits around Earth, that Earth orbits around the sun, and that eclipses occur when the moon passes through Earth's shadow from the sun. A total lunar eclipse occurs when all three celestial bodies are aligned, with Earth in the middle, and the moon cannot be seen from Earth. When eclipses happened in ancient times, primitive Chinese thought something was eating the moon. They decided the culprit had to be a dragon, because it could fly and was large and powerful enough to devour the moon. To save the moon, people would shout and bang drums to scare the dragon away. Because eclipses only last a short time, this fanciful tactic always worked, and its success reinforced the apparent truth of the myth for these primitive people.

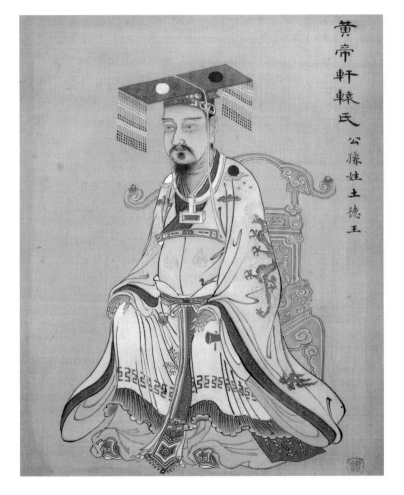

Yinglong, a rare winged dragon, helped the equally mythical Huangdi (pictured) defeat Chiyou for control of China.

Defense Against Evil Spirits

For centuries the Chinese people were deathly afraid of a wide variety of evil spirits that they believed freely roamed the earth with the intent of harming human beings. Their almost constant fear of such spirits led them to develop many ways to protect themselves. One way was in how they built their homes. Because the Chinese believed such spirits could only travel in a straight line, they often placed a wall directly in front of doorways to their homes to prevent spirits from entering. The same principle led them to plan many curves in the roads in China. Another defense against evil spirits is a mirror, which nullifies their power. Historian Susan D. Costello explains how using a mirror for protection works:

Mirrors were valued for ritual purposes associated with the power of reflection. Chinese spirits, both good and bad, are supposed to throng the earth and plague the living. Mirrors have the power to ward off evil since the form of any invisible spirit will become visible when reflected in the mirror. [Daoist] scholars are said to have worn a mirror hanging down their back so they could pursue their studies without fear of being harmed by the invisible spirits all around them. Nothing was considered more powerful in warding off these evil spirits than the threat of making them visible in the mirror. . . . In burial, mirrors were often placed face up on the breast of the deceased to protect them from evil spirits.

Susan D. Costello. "An Investigation of Early Chinese Bronze Mirrors at the Harvard University Art Museums." University of Texas at Austin, 2005. www.ischool.utexas.edu/~anagpic/pdfs/Costello.pdf.

There are many interesting myths about Chinese dragons, including how jade was created. One legend says that when the Mongols invaded China in the thirteenth century and overthrew the Jin dynasty, dragons were so sad that they began crying. When their tears struck the earth, they changed to jade, an ornamental stone that has always been highly valued in China. The myth that dragon tears could become a precious stone showed how much the Chinese valued such creatures.

Other Creatures

Chinese mythology includes other mystical creatures besides dragons. The Four Divine Creatures in Chinese mythology are Azure Dragon in the east, Vermillion Bird in the south, White Tiger in the west, and Black Tortoise in the north. Each of these mythical creatures guards one point of the compass to prevent harm from befalling China. They are also considered symbols of the four seasons: Azure Dragon for spring, Vermillion Bird for summer, White Tiger for autumn, and Black Tortoise for winter. Vermillion Bird is a graceful, elegant bird that resembles a peacock. It is usually depicted in flight with long flowing feathers trailing behind it. The Black Tortoise is also a symbol of longevity and is often depicted with a snake riding upon its shell because the snake is also associated with long life.

Snakes also figure prominently in several Chinese myths. Written in the fourth century B.C. by an anonymous author, *Shanhaijing* (*The Classic of Mountains and Seas*) is a history of China that is partially based on mythology. The ancient text catalogs various mythical creatures, including a giant snake called the bashe, whose waste is revered by doctors. According to *Shanhaijing*, "The Big Snake eats elephants and after three years it disgorges their bones. Gentlemen take a dose of this snake so that they will never have heart disease or illnesses of the belly. The snakes of Big Snake country are green, or yellow, or scarlet, or black. One author says the black snakes have a green head."[24]

A nobler creature than the bashe is the qilin, a one-horned animal similar to the unicorn, a horse-like creature with one horn growing out of its forehead that is popular in Western mythology. There are several Chinese myths about unicorn-like animals, and in some the qilin is referred to as the xiezhi. The qilin has a long, pointed horn growing out of its forehead like the unicorn, but descriptions of its body vary, with some accounts describing it as shaped like a lion, while others describe it as like a deer. One account says the qilin has green and blue scaly skin, hooves like a deer, the tail of an ox, and the head of a dragon. The qilin figures prominently in a myth about how writing began. The myth says that a qilin appeared before a Chinese emperor five thousand years ago with what appeared to be magic symbols on its back. The emperor copied them, and they became the first graphic representations of China's written language.

The qilin is also a symbol of justice. Because these mythical beasts can tell when people are lying, the early Chinese used them to settle disputes. The *Shuowen Jiezi*, a Chinese history from the second century B.C., explains how an emperor used a qilin for this purpose:

> When Gao Yao, administering justice, was doubtful about the guilt of a culprit, he ordered [the qilin] to butt it [run into the culprit with its horn]. It would butt the guilty, but spare the innocent. Accordingly, it was a sage [wise] animal born with one horn, a most efficient assistant in judicial proceedings. Therefore did Gao Yao hold it in high respect, using it on all occasions. Consequently, it belonged to the class of supernatural creatures of good omen.[25]

Evil Things

Along with those creatures that are helpful and good, Chinese mythology also has many supernatural characters that are evil, such as spirits and demons. When something terrible happened that primitive Chinese people could not explain, they reasoned that something evil caused it. Examples of such unexplained terrible incidents include the mysterious death of a loved one and storms that destroy crops of rice that people needed to keep from starving. DuBose writes, "[The] Chinese have been taught to consider themselves as constantly surrounded by a spirit world, invisible indeed and inaccessible to touch or handling, but none the less real, none the less influential [and filled with] billions of malevolent, malignant, and ruthless spirits to trouble them. [The] dread of spirits is the nightmare of the Chinaman's life."[26]

The Chinese believed in many types of evil entities, including animals that could assume human form. There were also the wandering spirits of people who had died but refused to leave Earth, including people who committed suicide by hanging themselves. Most of all, Chi-

Underwater Spirits

Underwater spirits (shui gui) are the ghosts of people who have drowned. They lurk in lakes and streams and try to drown other people so they can steal their bodies.

One tale about Yu the Great credits him with stopping a historic flood by defeating Wuzhiqi, a river demon in the form of a monkey, who was causing the flood.

nese people feared demons that could inhabit people, animals, and even natural objects, such as trees.

The story of the Red Child Demon is about a demon that assumes the form of a child tied to a tree, so it can lure people to their destruction. When the child-demon begins crying for help, a man passing by stops to help it. The demon then creates a whirlwind that takes the would-be rescuer away to his death. Demons are also associated with floods, which frequently devastated China throughout its long history. One tale tells of a river demon shaped like a monkey called Wuzhiqi that causes a historic flood. Yu the Great, a Chinese emperor and one of the most famous heroes in Chinese mythology, defeats Wuzhiqi and stops the flood.

How They Thought

Myths about eggs that create the world and demons that cause floods seem ridiculous today. But these strange tales are important, because they show how people long ago tried to understand the world around them. This is especially true in China, one of the first nations to begin recording its history. In her book *Chinese Mythology*, Anne Birrell writes, "The mythic narratives [stories] have remained preserved in amber, in their original context of works on history, philosophy, literature, political theory, and various [other papers] for over two millennia."[27] Thus, myths and other works provide a glimpse into the minds of people from the past.

CHAPTER 3

Gods and Goddesses

Many nations, such as Greece, have a small number of divine beings that are related and dominate the mythology of that country. China, however, may have more gods and goddesses than any other country in the world. Just one ancient book on Chinese myths, *Shanhaijing* (*The Classic of Mountains and Seas*), lists more than two hundred individual deities. In his book *Myths and Legends of China*, E.T.C. Werner writes, "The Chinese pantheon has gradually become so multitudinous that there is scarcely a being or thing which is not, or has not been at some time or other, propitiated or worshipped. As there are good and evil people in this world, so there are [good and bad] gods in the Otherworld."[28]

The huge universe of Chinese deities is populated by some of the strangest gods and goddesses of any of the world's mythologies. Ao Bing, one of several gods in charge of making it rain, has the head of a fish and the body of a human. Dou-mu is a goddess that has four heads with three eyes in each head and eight arms, four on each side of her body. Her multiple body parts help her in her immense task of recording the life and death of every person who ever lived. And Nu Choi is a goddess that ends droughts by setting herself on fire. Nu does not die, because she is immortal, but the burns she receives scar her so greatly that images often show Nu hiding her face with her hand or an article of clothing. Yu Huang is a mythical human emperor who becomes known as the Jade Emperor after he dies and ascends to Chinese heaven, where he becomes immortal and rules hundreds of

Yu Huang, top, center, was a mythical human emperor who became known as the Jade Emperor after he died and ascended to Chinese heaven.

other gods. While the ancient Chinese worshipped major gods, such as the Jade Emperor, they also worshipped minor gods, such as those that guarded their particular city or town and helped them to prosper.

The Chinese prayed to these major and minor gods for good health, wealth, rain for crops, success in love or war, and happiness. They built temples with statues of gods they worshipped and made offerings of food and burned incense to encourage the deities to help them. Incense was considered an especially efficient way to influence gods and goddesses. The Chinese believed the fragrant smoke would float all the way to heaven to please the divine beings that lived there.

Long Mu

One day a woman named Wen Shi found a beautiful white stone near a river and took it home. The stone was actually an egg containing five dragons, and when the egg hatched, Wen Shi raised the dragons. For this Wen Shi became the goddess Long Mu (mother of dragons).

Chinese Heaven

In addition to worshipping many different gods, the ancient Chinese also worshipped heaven itself. A belief in heaven was imbedded so deeply in Chinese culture that the Chinese expressed the importance of heaven in the shape of the coins they used. Until the Communists came to power in China in 1949, most Chinese coins were round with a square hole in the center. The round shape of the coin symbolized heaven and the square was Earth. Thus, the coins affirmed the Chinese belief that heaven surrounded them and played an important part in their lives.

However, the heaven those coins represented was unlike the mythological heaven of most nations and cultures. Heaven is usually a concept associated with religion. For Christians and Jews it is where God lives and where the souls of good people go when they die. Jannah is the Islamic version of a similar heaven, which is commonly referred to as paradise. According to Buddhism, there are several heavens and when people die they stay in them only temporarily before being reincarnated.

For the Chinese, heaven is not an eternal resting place for the dead. It is considered a sacred entity, separate from the deities that live there. In his book *The Dragon, Image, and Demon*, Hampden C. DuBose states that Chinese proverbs that people used in conversation show how they worshipped heaven in daily life. He writes,

> [Proverbs] are on every lip: "It is man's to scheme, it is Heaven's to accomplish;" "Nothing can escape the eye of Heaven;" "Man has a thousand schemes, but they are not equal to one scheme of Heaven;" "There is nothing partial in the ways of Heaven;" "Man does not know, but Heaven knows;" "You may deceive men, you cannot deceive Heaven;" [and] the most common proverb is, "We rely upon Heaven for our food."[29]

Worshipping heaven predated the birth of Confucianism, Daoism, and Buddhism in China and is connected to Shangdi, one of the first gods the Chinese worshipped. Oracle bone inscriptions show that Shangdi emerged as a god during the Shang dynasty in the second millennium B.C. Chinese mythologists believe that in the centuries after that, people began confusing the god Shangdi with heaven and thus began to consider heaven a separate entity. The result was that worship of Shangdi waned, and people began praying directly to heaven. The most important heaven worship was reserved for the emperor, who on certain days would perform lengthy rituals to persuade heaven to help his people.

Over many centuries the Chinese concept of heaven gradually evolved into being a place, where a multitude of gods lived. The Chinese believed those gods were organized in the same sort of bureaucracy in which the emperor and public officials governed them on earth.

A Celestial Bureaucracy

The ancient Chinese had a need to establish order in how they believed their world worked, and this influenced the development of Chinese mythology. Creation myths, for example, explain how the world and its people were brought forth out of *hundun* (chaos). In a similar manner, the Chinese tried to create an orderly framework to explain the activities of the many gods and goddesses they had invented over several thousands of years.

A Heavenly Bureaucracy

In the article "The Spirits of Chinese Religion," on the Brooklyn College website, mythologist Stephen F. Teiser explains why the ancient Chinese believed that the hierarchy of deities they worshipped functioned the same way government officials did. He writes,

For many years it has been a truism that the Chinese conception of gods is based on the Chinese bureaucracy, that the social organization of the human government is the essential model that Chinese people use when imagining the gods. At the apex of the divine bureaucracy stands the Jade Emperor (Yuhuang dadi) in Heaven, corresponding to the human Son of Heaven (Tianzi, another name for emperor) who rules over Earth. The Jade Emperor is in charge of an administration divided into bureaus. Each bureaucrat-god takes responsibility for a clearly defined domain or discrete function. The local officials of the celestial administration are the Gods of Walls and Moats, and below them are the Gods of the Hearth, one per family, who generate a never-ending flow of reports on the people under their jurisdiction. They are assisted in turn by gods believed to dwell inside each person's body, who accompany people through life and into death, carrying with them the records of good and evil deeds committed by their charges. The very lowest officers are those who administer punishment to deceased spirits passing through the purgatorial chambers of the underworld. They too have reports to fill out, citizens to keep track of, and jails to manage.

Stephen F. Teiser. "The Spirits of Chinese Religion." Brooklyn College, 1996. http://acc6.its.brooklyn.cuny.edu/~phalsall/texts/lopez.html.

When China became unified in 221 B.C., its leaders established a rigid, highly structured bureaucracy to control the vast number of people within its borders. The emperor was the nation's most powerful person, but the nation was actually run by tens of thousands of government officials who worked in various jobs at different levels of government throughout China. Gaozu, the first Han dynasty emperor, established this civil-service system in 207. People were appointed to jobs based on results of academic tests that proved they were worthy to hold those positions. There were nine different levels of government service. The top officials headed these various ministries (sections of government) and reported directly to the emperor.

The Chinese so deeply revered this system that they imagined that gods and goddesses belonged to a similar hierarchy. In his book *Introducing Chinese Religions*, Mario Poceski, a professor of Chinese religions at the University of Florida, explains that the Chinese imagined that gods worked together in heaven to regulate life on Earth in the same way government officials ruled their daily lives. He writes, "Like its earthly counterpart, the celestial bureaucracy is structured hierarchically, with each of its members occupying a specific place and performing circumscribed functions. The whole bureaucratic structure is based on established rules and procedures, and written records are carefully kept by appropriate officials."[30]

Heavenly Bureaucrats

The celestial bureaucracy of gods the Chinese invented essentially established the gods as workers in offices responsible for everything on Earth from thunder and lightning to health, personal prosperity, and even literature. Lei Gong (whose name means God of Thunder in English) is in charge of thunder; he uses a drum and hammer to produce noise. His assistants include Dian Mu (Mother of Lightning), who uses mirrors to send bolts of lightning into the sky, and Yun Tong (Cloud Youth), who pushes clouds speedily across the sky during storms. People even believed gods and goddesses in different heavenly offices wore clothing similar to that of their earthly counterparts.

When people prayed to these divine bureaucrats for help, such as for rain to end a drought, they offered them ritual sacrifices of food and other things. The sacrifices were similar to bribes they would give to real public officials when requesting a favor. In her book *Confucianism*, religious studies professor Jennifer Oldstone-Moore writes, "[The heavenly bureaucrats] are approached and petitioned in the same way as human officials—because they are just as susceptible to bribes and favors."[31] Many other cultures also gave offerings to the deities they worshipped in order to win their favor. The Chinese, however, raised this form of heavenly bribery to a fine art. They offered up not only prayers but also placed food before images of gods and burned paper spirit money. The

Lei Gong was the Chinese thunder god.

Chinese did this because giving people gifts to gain their help or favor was something that was part of daily life in China. This cultural trait of giving something to get something in return continues in China to the present day.

Culture-Bearing Gods

Making a fire and using it to cook food or stay warm and growing crops for food seem like absurdly simple tasks to modern people. However, primitive people did not know how to do these things. While they gradually learned for themselves how to create fire, grow crops, and do many other things, the ancient Chinese still credited gods for showing them how to do these vital tasks. Examples of such gods are Sui Ren, the god of fire, and Shennong, the god of farming.

In her book *Chinese Mythology*, mythologist Anne Birrell calls such Chinese gods "culture bearers" and writes, "[Importance in such myths] is attached to the concern the gods feel for the physical well-being and nourishment of humans and to the great care they take to teach and show humans how to perform the cultural act."[32] Although these myths say the gods taught people how to do things, they actually honor the primitive people who were the first to learn how to do these vital tasks by using the stories to transform them into gods.

Guan Yu became the war god Guandi.

Most culture-bearing gods are male, as are the vast majority of Chinese deities, because for thousands of years China was a male-dominated society in which women had little social standing. Some male gods were mortals who were elevated to divine status for having culturally important traits like bravery in battle and loyalty. One of them was Guandi, who started life as Guan Yu, a man who lived in the third century and became famous for his bravery and loyalty as a soldier. As a youth, Guan was passing a house when he heard a woman crying. When he asked what was wrong, he found out she was unhappy because a rich man was going to force her to become his concubine (mistress). Guan decided to kill the man to save the woman's virtue. He knew he would have to flee for his life, because the man's family was powerful. But gods intervened and made his face red, allowing Guan to escape. In his book *Chinese Gods: An Introduction to Chinese Folk Religion*, Jonathan Chamberlain writes, "As [Guan] was wondering how he would be able to [get away] without being recognized, he stopped to wash his face in a mountain stream. There he caught sight of his face, which had turned red. He presented himself to the officers at the pass knowing they would not recognize him, told them his name was Kuan, and got through."[33] Guan later became one of several gods of war, and he is easily recognizable in images because he is always shown with a bright red face.

Another human who became a deity was Zhang Lang, a man who cruelly abandoned his wife for a younger woman. Heaven punished Zhang by making him blind, which forced him to become a beggar. Years later when Zhang went to a home to beg for food, a woman cooked a wonderful meal for him and treated him nicely. Zhang was so touched by her kindness that he told her how he had become blind. Crying, he also told her how sorry he was for what he had done to his wife. The woman then admitted she was the wife he had left and told him to open his eyes. His sight miraculously restored, Zhang recognized her. But he was so overcome with shame that he leaped into the blazing kitchen fire and burned to death.

This act of repentance so impressed the gods that they made Zhang the kitchen god, known as Zao Jun. The myth

The Archery God

Yi the Archer, also known as Houyi, is one of the most famous and heroic gods in Chinese mythology. The best-known tale about Yi explains how he saved the earth from being burned up by too many suns. The earth once had ten suns that were actually sons of the god Dijun. They resembled three-legged crows and were called sun birds. Dijun's sons lived in a mulberry tree, and each day Dijun allowed one of them to travel around the earth to provide light and warmth for people. One day all ten sun birds decided to fly at the same time. The resulting heat from so many suns began burning up the earth. In the book *Teach Yourself: Chinese Myths*, author Te Lin explains, "The heat seared the ground, rivers turned to vapor and the crops became ashes. Even the rocks began to melt." Dijun realized that by dis-obeying his order his sons would destroy the world and everyone living in it. So Dijun sent the archery god Yi to correct the problem. Yi, accompanied by his wife, Chang'e, used his bow and arrows to shoot nine of the sun birds out of the sky and save the world and its people. Instead of rewarding Yi, Dijun was so upset over the death of his sons that he punished Yi and his wife. He made them mortal and ordered them to leave heaven and live on earth. According to Te Lin, Dijun said, "Alas, nine of my sons are dead. Yi, you did as I asked, it is true. But I can no longer bear to look upon you, and be reminded of my dear ones who are dead. You and your wife Chang'e must leave Heaven, leave my side forever."

Te Lin. *Teach Yourself: Chinese Myths*. Chicago: Contemporary Books, 2001, pp. 15, 16.

The god Dijun (shown) punished Yi the Archer and his wife by making them mortal.

of Zao Jun is designed as a morality tale to instruct people how to act properly, in this case being faithful in marriage. As the god of kitchens, Zao watches over the safety of families and especially fire in the home, which provides vital heat to warm people and cook food. Zao Jun also has another duty. Once a year before the Chinese New Year, he reported to the Jade Emperor on the behavior of people living in the home. In an attempt to bribe Zao Jun to give them a good report, family members prayed to an image of him, left offerings of sweets, and smeared honey on his lips. In his book *The Medical Missionary*, John Harvey Kellogg cited the prayer, which includes these verses:

> God, god of the kitchen,
> Come, here is your pudding
> And here is your t'ang (sugar).
> Go flit up to heaven,
> Be done in a trice,
> Forget all the bad,
> Tell only what's nice.[34]

People tried to keep Zao Jun happy by putting up new pictures of him each year during the New Year festival. The Chinese did the same thing to honor door gods called *men-shen*, which are among the oldest deities in Chinese mythology. The images of the gods protecting the entrance to homes are those of fierce warriors dressed in armor and carrying weapons. Their frightening appearance is supposed to keep evil spirits from entering homes.

Goddesses

Although the majority of deities are male, the ancient Chinese also worshipped many goddesses, including several that are very powerful and beloved throughout China. Nu Kua, the creator of the first human beings, is one of China's most popular and revered goddesses. Her importance is seen in a myth in which she saves the world from destruction. According to the myth, an evil male god named Gong Gong tries to destroy the world by knocking down the four pillars that hold it up. Nu Kua replaces the four damaged pillars and saves the world. The second-century-B.C. book *Huainanzi* (*The Masters/Philosophers of Huainan*) tells what happened: "Fires flamed without being extinguished, waters inundated without being stopped, fierce beasts ate the people, and birds of prey seized the old and weak in their claws. [Then Nu Kua] fused together stones of the five colors with which to patch together [and hold up] azure heaven, and cut off the feet of a turtle to re-set the four pillars."[35]

Despite the immense power attributed to Nu Kua for both creating humans and saving Earth from destruction, this goddess's exalted standing is an exception in China's populous divine universe. Birrell explains, "There are fewer goddesses in the classical Chinese pantheon than gods, and with a few exceptions, goddesses are not equal in importance to the gods in term of function, cult, or continuity of mythological tradition."[36] The status of goddesses mirrors the inferior social status women held throughout most of China's long history. In the past, women were usually denied a formal education. When they married, they became the property of their husbands and were rarely allowed to leave their homes. Under communism, however, women in China in the twentieth century won equality with men.

Xi Wangmu, which in Chinese means Queen Mother of the West, is another powerful goddess. Her revered standing as a mother figure is evident in her name. *Mu* means "mother" and *wang* means "sovereign." She is one of the oldest Chinese deities; the first historical mention of her is on an oracle bone inscription from the Shang dynasty thirty-three centuries ago. It reads, "If we make offering to the Western Mother there will be approval."[37] Xi Wangmu lives on Kunlun Mountain, a mythical sacred place where many Chinese gods live, and she has control over the life and death of all humans. Xi even has the power to make human beings immortal. Birrell writes, "The major attribute of the Queen Mother of the West is her power to confer immortality. [She] is pictured in traditional iconography [sacred portraiture] holding her staff (scepter or wand)

Gong Gong

Gong Gong was a god blamed for a flood that nearly destroyed the world. Images of Gong Gong portray him as a black dragon, and he is often shown with a nine-headed snake.

Mazu, the goddess of the sea, could see the future and had the ability to change it.

in her left hand and a basket of the peaches of immortality in the other. The peaches were fabled to ripen only once every three thousand years."[38]

Mazu, the goddess of the sea, was human when she was born on Meizhou Island in China's Fujian Province in about 960 during the Song dynasty. When she was born, the room she was in became filled with light and the scent of flowers. Her name at birth was Lin Moniang, and she had the supernatural power to see the future and to change it. Lin's father was a fisherman and almost drowned at sea during a typhoon when Lin was a young girl.

As Lin grew older, she refused to marry because all she wanted to do was help people. She predicted weather, which was important for fishermen, and also had the power to heal sick people. When Lin was twenty-eight years old, she was magically transformed into the goddess Mazu. In "Mazu: Goddess of the Sea," an article on the GBTimes website written by Terhi Mikkolainen, it is said that

> she went to the top of the mountains and disappeared in the mist, at about the same time that a rainbow appeared. People interpreted this to mean that Lin was now a [goddess] who lived among men to help them in times of trouble. Many seafarers over the course of the centuries have told of seeing a woman in a red dress or surrounded by light who appears in the middle of the sea to warn the voyagers of an approaching storm.[39]

People who made their living from the sea began to pray to Mazu to keep them safe and allow them to catch many fish.

Destroyers

Most Chinese gods and goddesses, such as Mazu, help people, but some cause destruction, and they are known as destroyer gods or goddesses. One is the goddess Nuba. She is one of the most feared divine beings, because she creates drought. Nuba is the daughter of Huangdi, the mythical Yellow Emperor of Chinese mythology. When her father fought with the god Chiyou, Nuba created dry conditions to neutralize a storm created by two of Chiyou's allies, wind god Feng Bo and rain god Yu Shi. After this legendary battle, Nuba stayed on Earth instead of returning to heaven. Wherever Nuba wandered, she caused dry conditions, and droughts were calamities to the Chinese because most people were farmers. Instead of worshipping Nuba, the Chinese feared her. *Shanhaijing* explains how people tried to end drought by praying for her to leave so it could rain again: "The Goddess of Drought (Nuba) often flees from place to place. Every place she goes people want to chase her away. They command her, 'Goddess, go back north!'"[40] Images of Nuba show her as bald and dressed in green.

Huangdi's enemy Chiyou is one of the oldest and strangest gods in Chinese mythology. *Chiyou* is a Chinese word

The Moon Maid

When the ancient Chinese looked at the moon, they imagined Chang'e lived there. Chang'e is the wife of Yi the Archer. They had both been deities that lived in heaven until the god Dijun punished them by making them mortal and banishing them to Earth. Chang'e was unhappy as a mortal. Unknown to her, Yi had obtained a pill to become immortal. According to E.T.C. Werner in his book Myths and Legends of China, *this is what happened when Chang'e found and ate the pill Yi had hidden:*

[She] suddenly felt [as] if she had wings [and] opened the window and flew out. [She] continued her flight until she reached a luminous sphere [the moon], shining like glass, of enormous size, and very cold. No living being was to be seen. All of a sudden she began to cough, and vomited the covering of the pill of immortality, which was changed into a rabbit as white as the purest jade.

Like many Chinese myths, there are different versions of this tale of the woman who lives in the moon. One version claims Chang E was always human but still stole the pill from Yi, who had been given it as a reward. In another version the elixir is liquid but she only drinks half of it, which is why she can only fly to the moon and not as far as heaven. A third version claims that when Chang E gained immortality the gods would not allow her to return to heaven and made her live on the moon. Even her name kept changing. She was also known as Chang Er, Change-O, Heng E, and Heng-O.

E.T.C. Werner. *Myths and Legends of China.* New York: Dover, 1994, pp. 184–185.

Chang'e flies to the moon after she ate Yt the Archer's immortality pill.

for reptile, and this god is sometimes depicted as having the feet of a tortoise and head of a snake. Other versions of myths about Chiyou say he has a bronze head, a metal forehead, and horns. He also has four eyes and six arms, each of which wields a weapon during battle. One reason Chiyou is considered a god of war is that his followers say he invented weapons to wage war.

The most famous myth about Chiyou involves his battle with Huangdi. In various versions of this epic fight, Chiyou is hard to beat because he is able to use his horns to butt people aside; he is also able to fly over opposing forces. One version says that when Chiyou leads mythical animals against Huangdi, the Yellow Emperor has his solders blow horns that sound like dragons to scare them away. According to another tale, Chiyou uses fog to confuse Huangdi's army, so the emperor invents the compass and leads his troops to safety. In all the versions, however, Huangdi triumphs and kills Chiyou. Huangdi fears his slain opponent so much that he cuts off his head and buries it separately from his body to make sure Chiyou can never return to fight him again.

Other destroyer gods include Drum, another god that causes drought, and Lu Yueh, a god that causes epidemics. The ancient Chinese believed disease, especially widespread epidemics, were sent by heaven. Lu was responsible for sending seasonal illnesses. As expected of a god that creates disaster, Lu looks quite horrible: He has a blue face, red hair, and three eyes, and he carries a sword coated with plague and a flag with the symbol for plague on it.

CHAPTER 4

Confucianism, Daoism, and Buddhism

The three main Chinese religions are Confucianism, Daoism, and Buddhism. They are known collectively as *sanjiao*, which means "three teachings." The Chinese group them together because all three religions formulate a moral code designed to help people lead better lives. Followers of other religions, such as Judaism, Christianity, and Islam, almost always devote themselves exclusively to one god that is at the center of their faith and refuse to worship other gods or to accept teachings from other religions. Throughout history, this lack of tolerance toward people who do not worship their god or gods or share their beliefs has resulted in violence between Jews, Christians, Muslims, and followers of other religions. This religious warfare continues in modern times with armed conflicts between Protestant and Roman Catholic Christians in Northern Ireland and between Shia Muslims and Sunni Muslims in the Middle East.

Such religious intolerance has mainly been absent in China, where Confucianism, Daoism, and Buddhism have peacefully coexisted for more than two thousand years alongside folk religion, which is even older. In his book *The Dragon, Image, and Demon*, Hampden C. DuBose comments on this harmonious coexistence. He writes, "It seems to make little difference to the people to what temple they go or what god they worship."[41]

China's Three Teachings

One reason for the lack of conflict between various Chinese religions is that none of them restrict people from worshipping various deities. The second reason for this religious harmony is that Chinese people are willing to accept moral values on how to live their lives from more than one religion. In an article for the journal *Worldviews*, Daniel J. Paracka Jr., a professor at Kennesaw State University in Kennesaw, Georgia, and an expert on Chinese culture, explains how this harmonious relationship works:

> It has been common practice for people in China to embrace all three [religious] traditions in order to take from each whatever they need under varied circumstances. A common example to describe this practice tells of a man who has to study hard to pass the civil service examination (Confucianism). Before the exam he visits a Buddhist temple to pray to pass the exam (Buddhism), and if he felt nervous or ill he would ask a Daoist monk for herbal medicine (Daoism).[42]

Folk religion began thousands of years ago in the prehistoric period, when the Chinese first began inventing myths and deities to explain what was happening in the world around them. Folk religion is sometimes called *shenism,* from the Chinese word *shen*, which means "spirit" or "god." This simplistic religion focuses on how various gods, goddesses, and spirits, including those of dead people, cause drought or flooding, sickness, war, and the bad or good luck everyone occasionally experiences.

Folk religion initiated the belief that people should worship the spirits of their dead ancestors, a practice that became an important part of Chinese culture. This belief is based on the concept that people have an eternal soul that can be kept alive through sacrifices performed by male family members. With proper sacrifices, ancestors become deities that have the power to positively influence what happens

A shen, or spirit, of happiness prominent in Chinese folklore. The Chinese people believed that these spirits could cause good or bad luck.

to their descendants. However, when people fail to make sacrifices to their ancestors, the ancestors become demons that haunt their descendants.

Confucianism and Daoism began in China about twenty-five hundred years ago, while Buddhism originated in India and came to China in the first century A.D. These three faiths believe in many of the same gods, goddesses, and spirits of folk religion, and they also adopted the belief that people should worship the spirits of their dead ancestors from folk religion. However, these newer Chinese religions also created philosophies to help people live better lives. In this regard, they are similar to the Ten Commandments in the Bible, which is a moral guide that teaches people right from wrong.

The Founder of Confucianism

Although few details about his life are known, Confucius, the founder of Confucianism, is believed to have been a real person. Born with the name Kong Qui in 551 B.C. in Lu, a feudal state that is the present-day province of Shandong in southwestern China, Confucius traveled and taught throughout China until he died in 479 B.C. Because he was so respected as a teacher and philosopher in his later years, people called him Kong Fuzi, an honorary title that means "Master Kong." Roman Catholic Jesuit missionaries who introduced his ideas to the rest of the world in the sixteenth century latinized his name to Confucius.

Many historians consider Confucius to be one of the most influential thinkers and teachers in world history and often compare him to the great Greek philosopher Socrates. Some historians also claim that Confucius had a greater impact on Chinese history and culture than any other single person. In his book *The Way of Confucius*, Jonathan Price writes, "Confucius has probably had a greater influence on more people and over a longer time than any other comparable figure in the history of the world."[43]

In general Confucius taught a set of moral principles that helped people live good lives. He summed up a simple for-

The inscription in this scroll painting is a quote from Confucius's Analects, a set of moral principles that helped people live righteously.

mula for how people should live when he wrote, "What I do not wish men to do to me, I also wish not to do to men" and "What you do not want done to yourself, do not do to others."[44] This teaching is similar to the Golden Rule, a belief that is the core of moral instruction for many of the world's religions. However, Confucius's impact on Chinese history and culture also comes from the strict moral code he developed regarding personal relationships.

Confucianism

Confucius created a rigid social structure based on *ren*, which means "compassion" or "loving others." His writings describe five social bonds that people have to honor in order to lead good lives. They are ruler to ruled, father to son, husband to wife, elder brother to younger brother, and friend to friend. Confucius believed family is the most important bond in life, which is illustrated by three of his five bonds. Confucianism was so influential in shaping the way people thought that family relationships became the most important relationships in the lives of Chinese people.

Confucius also stressed the importance of the relationship between people and government. He believed that people should respect government, and this teaching had a huge impact on Chinese culture. It influenced the Chinese to have unquestioning loyalty to their emperor and other officials who wielded power over them. Although Confucius also said that officials had to be fair and just in performing their duties, his ideal of strict, unwavering allegiance to the ruling government helped keep China stable for centuries. During the Han dynasty (206 B.C. to A.D. 220), its emperors even adopted his ideas, which had become known as Confucianism, as China's official philosophy. In an article in the journal *Focus on Asian Studies*, historian Judith A. Berling writes, "From that time [Han dynasty] on the imperial state promoted Confucian values to maintain law, order, and the status quo."[45]

In 195 B.C. Han emperor Gaozu admired Confucius so much that he offered a sacrifice to him at his tomb in Qufu. This worship of Confucius continued in other parts of China, and the first temple devoted to him was built in

Compatible Chinese Religions

When Christian missionary Hampden C. DuBose went to China in 1872, he was amazed that most Chinese participated in more than one religion. DuBose believed it was wrong for people to worship multiple gods from multiple religions. And followers of other major religions, such as Jews and Muslims, shared that sentiment. In his book The Dragon, Image, and Demon, *DuBose describes how the Chinese had no trouble moving between the three main Chinese religions of Confucianism, Daoism, and Buddhism:*

Many of the gods [in the three religions] are the same. In a Buddhist temple there are seen Taoist [Daoist] images, and in a Taoist temple Buddhist divinities are enshrined. The Buddhists call the goddess of Mercy "the great teacher to open the gate," and the Taoists call her "The self-existent Heaven-honored." The Pearly Emperor is called "Imperial Ruler" by the Taoists, and "King of Indra's Paradise" by the Buddhists. The Confucianists call the god of War "Military Sage," the Buddhists call him the "God of Protection," and the Taoists call him the "Minister of Heaven." [Religion] in the heart of a Chinese is three-headed, and so [they look] for help on every side. All are Confucianists, all Buddhists, all Taoists.

Hampden C. DuBose. *The Dragon, Image, and Demon.* London: S.W. Partridge, 1886. http://ia700202.us.archive .org/15/items/thedragonimage00dubouoft/thedragon image00dubouoft.pdf.

480 in his hometown of Qufu in Shandong Province. Thus, the creator of what was intended as only a moral philosophy became a deity in a new religion. This happened even though Confucius was not particularly religious and was ambivalent about the need to worship divine beings.

The Founder of Daoism

Laozi is recognized as the founder of Daoism, but no one knows whether he was even a real person. The first historical reference to Laozi appears in *Shiji* (*Records of the Grand Historian of China*), a history written by Siam Qian in the first century B.C. The book says that Laozi lived at the same time as Confucius and that the two once met and argued philosophy. Other historical sources claim Laozi lived in either the fourth, fifth, or sixth century B.C.; even his name is not known because Laozi is actually an honorary title that means "The Old Master." Laozi is also credited with writing the Dao De Jing (The Classic of the Dao and Virtue), a classic text central to philosophical and religious Daoism, but some scholars believe it is a compilation of Daoist writings by many people. There is also no consensus on when this classic Chinese text was written, with estimates varying from the fourth to the sixth century B.C. In a paper for Early Chinese Thought, a class at Indiana University–Bloomington in 2010, Robert Eno, the professor of the class, comments on works about Daoism:"Daoist texts sound deeply profound, while Confucians have a tendency to seem shallow and pedantic. One of the great attractions of Daoist texts is actually that the sense of wisdom they convey is so deep that it frequently seems impossible to understand what they mean."[46]

Confucianism deals with easily understood concepts, such as conducting relationships with other people, so it can seem simplistic compared with Daoism, which deals with abstract ideas, such as the nature of life itself. Daoists claim the goal of people should be to understand the *Dao*, the basic, primal life force that infuses people, animals, and nature and shapes everything that happens. However, Laozi and other Daoist sages express the nature of Dao in such mystical terms that it is difficult to understand what it is. These lines from the Dao De Jing's first chapter show the complexity of Daoist thought: "The Dao of the universe comes from nothing, with no beginning and no ending. The Universe, the Mother of the World gives birth and names to all things. To follow the Nothingness of Dao, we possess the wonder of all things around us."[47]

Despite being hard to comprehend, Daoist ideas are basic to Chinese philosophy and culture. One concept is yin and yang, the belief that dualities exist in human nature and in the world itself, such as good and evil, light and dark, strong and weak, and male and

The Eight Immortals

The Eight Immortals were eight humans who became immortal by following Daoist practices to be healthy and live a long life. Daoists created them to show the power of their religion. There were six men (Li Tiegual, Zhongli Quan, Cao Guojio, Han Xiang, Lu DongBin, and Zhang Guolo) and two women (Lan Caihe and He Xiangu).

female. A Daoist symbol for this concept is a circle divided into curved halves. Daoists believe that understanding how opposites act and react in daily life helps people understand how to follow the Dao. Another Daoist concept is *wu-wei*, or "nondoing." A central principle of Daoism is to do nothing to affect the natural course of events, because they represent the flow of Dao. This does not mean being passive all the time but making sure that whatever action one takes is logical and aligns with the natural way things should occur.

Daoism and China

Daoism became a religion when Daoists began to worship Laozi as they did other gods and goddesses. They did this because according to Daoism, Laozi never died. Instead, Daoists believe he wandered away after discovering how to become immortal and continues to live even today. This myth about Laozi's immortality led people to believe they themselves could also live forever. They thought they could do that by following Daoist practices that include meditation, deep-breathing techniques, a nourishing diet, and physical exercises.

The Daoist emphasis on achieving long life led to the creation of two major areas of Chinese culture: medicine and the martial arts. Much of Chinese medicine, including acupuncture, is based on the idea of qi (chi), an energy Chinese doctors believe flows through every living thing. Daoist theory says that people become sick when the natural flow of chi in their bodies is disrupted or blocked. In acupuncture doctors try to restore the proper flow of qi by inserting needles in certain areas of the body that eliminate whatever is blocking the flow of this vital life force. The idea of balancing yin-yang elements in the body, including the food people eat, also became central to Chinese medical treatments.

Foo Dogs

Almost every religious temple, royal palace, and government building in China was once guarded by a stone or metal representation of a lion known as *shishi*. The shishi are known in the West as foo dogs, because they are closely associated with Buddhist temples. Fo is the Chinese name for the Buddha, the god Buddhists worship.

Laozi, depicted here riding his buffalo, is credited with writing the Dao De Jing, a classic text central to philosophical and religious Daoism, although some scholars claim it is a compilation of writings by many people.

Daoist exercises influenced the development of Chinese martial arts. Hua Tuo, a famous second-century Daoist physician, is credited with developing exercises that mimic the movements of five animals—a tiger, a deer, a monkey, a bear, and a bird. Some of these exercises evolved into martial arts techniques. Daoism is also directly connected to taijiquan, or "supreme ultimate fist," a martial art known in the West as tai chi. Taijiquan is based on Daoist theories about strengthening qi. It became both a martial art and a form of exercise that promotes health and is especially helpful for the elderly.

Buddhism

Unlike Daoism and Confucianism, Buddhism is the only one of the three teachings that is not native to China. It originated in India about 560 B.C. from the teachings of Siddhartha Gautama, who became known as the Buddha, which means "the awakened one" in Sanskrit, an ancient Indian language. When Buddhist missionaries came to China to spread their religion in the first century A.D., they continued to practice their physical exercises to stay healthy. Many of the exercises mimicked the natural movements of animals, and from them

Religion and Philosophy

According to author Kenneth C. Davis, Confucianism and Daoism were important in shaping Chinese history and culture because of the philosophies of living that the two religions teach. Davis believes the two religions were powerful in influencing Chinese thought throughout China's long history even though their philosophies are very different. Confucianism promotes the sanctity of family ties and the right of the emperor to rule, while Daoism preaches the need for people to lead lives that do not interrupt the natural flow of events as dictated by the Dao. In his book Don't Know Much About Mythology, *Davis writes,*

The two great strains of native Chinese philosophy, Confucianism and [Daoism]—both introduced around 500 B.C.—clearly shaped China's history, government, and culture more than any myth or religious beliefs by emphasizing social order, loyalty to family and king, and ancestor worship. Confucianism is a moral code of proper behavior designed to achieve an ideally gentle world in which every individual has a place within the family and every family has a place within the society. Confucianism places the virtue of a disciplined communal order above the need to appease the gods, while [Daoism], the second major school of Chinese thinking, stresses the importance of individuals living simply and close to nature."

Kenneth C. Davis. *Don't Know Much About Mythology: Everything You Need to Know About the Greatest Stories in Human History but Never Learned.* New York: Harper-Collins, 2005, pp. 362–363.

some of China's most famous martial arts developed, including *shaolin, hung gar,* and *wing chun.*

Despite its connection to martial arts, Buddhism is a gentle religion that promotes inner peace and harmony with all people. The Buddha claimed that people suffered because they desired what they could not have, such as health when they were ill, youth when they were old, or wealth when they were poor. He said people could end their suffering by eliminating their desire for things they could not obtain. Techniques Buddhists use to eliminate desire include viewing reality as it is and not as it appears to be, never harming anyone else, and making a constant effort to improve their attempts to live a good life. Buddhists also believed in reincarnation, the idea that they will continue to be born again and again so they can continue their personal struggle to achieve perfection.

Buddhism quickly spread throughout China, and several emperors adopted it as the state religion. One of the reasons Buddhism became popular is that it is similar in many ways to Daoism. Both religions have elements of mysticism and focus on meditation to help people control their emotions and their reactions to what happens to them in the course of their daily lives. In addition, both Daoism and Buddhism, unlike the more conservative Confucianism, welcome worship of an elaborate pantheon of deities as part of their religious activities.

Confucius supported rituals and sacrifices to various gods because he believed the practices stabilized society by making people feel secure because their gods were protecting them. However, Confucius was wary of depending too much on deities and wrote, "One should revere the ghosts and gods but keep your distance [from them]."[48] Daoism and Buddhism, however, freely worship many gods, goddesses,

A statue of Siddhartha Gautama, who became the Buddha, or "awakened one." Buddhist missionaries came to China from India in the first century A.D.

and spirits. However, early Daoists and Buddhists sometimes altered the mythology of some of the deities that had existed before Daoism and Buddhism, and they even added new ones to conform to their religious philosophies.

Religious Mythology

Daoism is the closest of the three teachings to folk religion, because it freely accepts the mythological beings many Chinese were worshipping before Daoism was created. Historian Joan Chan says Daoists even expanded the pantheon of deities to attract followers. In an article for *China Eye* magazine, she writes, "For thousands of years these clever high priests created a fantasy playground for all ages and all classes to worship Laozi as their god alongside numerous other immortals, ghosts, and sacred animals such as the monkey and dragon."[49]

To bolster their religious beliefs, Daoists created a myth about three gods that exemplify the perfection people can reach by learning to interpret the Dao and follow it to lead better lives. This trinity of sacred beings is called by different names, such as the Three Pure Ones, the Three Divine Teachers, and the Three Clarities. They are considered so sacred that only Daoist priests are allowed to petition them for blessings. Among the older deities the Daoists chose to worship were Xi Wangmu, the Queen Mother of the West, and the Jade Emperor.

Daoists also added several new figures to the pantheon of Chinese gods to promote their beliefs. Perhaps the strangest, and certainly one of the most beloved, is the Monkey King. Sun Wukong was a monkey that was born from a stone. He later acquired human intelligence and superhuman powers through Daoist practices that perfected this mind and body, and he became king of all the monkeys in the world.

Sun is a main character in *Hsi-yu Chi* (*The Journey to the West*), a sixteenth-century classical novel written by Wu Cheng'en. In this work, Sun learns his lessons from Daoist founder Laozi. In the following passage from the book, Sun begs Laozi to be his teacher:

"Master! Please accept this humble seeker as your disciple!" said the Monkey King, dropping to his knees and knocking his head on the floor before a man who looked as old as Heaven, yet strong and healthy.

Sun Wukong was a monkey who was born from a stone. He later acquired human intelligence and superhuman powers through Daoist practices that perfected his mind and body and thus became king of all the monkeys in the world.

[Laozi] asked the Monkey King, "What is your name?" "I have no name, Master, for I had no parents to give me one. I was born from a magic stone," said the Monkey King. Well, what if I name you [Sun Wukong]?" So, the Monkey King became a student of [Daoism].[50]

One of the lessons the Monkey King learned was how to change himself into anything he wanted and fly through the air by somersaulting from cloud to cloud. The final lesson was how to become immortal, the goal of Daoists. The Monkey King is the subject of many myths, most of which revolve around his volatile, fun-loving nature, which continually gets him into trouble. The superhero monkey became a symbol of how Daoism could perfect the negative parts of humanity, even in a monkey. The name Laozi gave him is evidence of that. One of the many meanings for the word *sun* in Chinese is "monkey," and *wukong* means "awareness of emptiness."

The close, amiable relationship between Daoism and Buddhism is showcased in *Hsi-yu Chi*. After gaining his

Ancestor Worship

Ancestor worship has been part of Chinese culture since prehistoric times. It has also been a central part of the religious practices of every Chinese religion for several thousands of years. The ancient Chinese believed that people had several souls and that when people died, their souls remained on Earth as spirits. They also believed that the spirits of their ancestors would help them in their daily lives if they made offerings to them and kept their memory alive. To do this, families kept a list of names of their ancestors on spirit tablets, which they placed on altars in their homes. According to the article "Settling the Dead: Funerals, Memorials, and Beliefs Concerning the Afterlife" on the Living in the Chinese Cosmos website, families made sacrifices of food and spirit money to their ancestors to keep them happy. The article states,

S acrificial rites consisted of daily or bimonthly devotions and anniversary services. Families burned incense every day on the domestic ancestral altar, which houses the family spirit tablets in hierarchical order. In front of the tablets often glowed an eternal flame, symbol of the ancestor's abiding presence within the household. Anniversary rites took place on the death date of each major deceased member of the family. Sacrificial food was offered, and living members of the family participated in the ceremony in ritual order based on age and generation. Sacrifices were also made to the ancestors during major festival periods and on important family occasions such as births and weddings. In general, these domestic devotions reflected a ritual apparatus characteristic of most other forms of Chinese religious practice.

Living in the Chinese Cosmos. "Settling the Dead: Funerals, Memorials, and Beliefs Concerning the Afterlife." http://afe .easia.columbia.edu/cosmos/prb/journey.htm.

Ancestor worship has been a central part of all Chinese religions. Pictured here is a commemorative plaque of a loved one.

unique powers, Sun helps legendary Buddhist priest Xuan-zang go to India, so he could bring sacred Buddhist texts to China. Buddhism also adopted or invented its share of gods and goddesses, including Yama, the god of death, and Hotei, the god of happiness and luck.

Another link between the two religions is Guanyin, the Buddhist goddess of mercy; she is also revered by Daoists. Historians say Guanyin is the transplanted Chinese version of an earlier and similar Buddhist deity from India. Whatever her origin, Guanyin is immensely popular, because people believe she is compassionate and merciful. In most Guanyin myths, she is a mortal who becomes a goddess after she ascends to heaven. In his book *Myths and Legends of China*, mythologist E.T.C. Werner explains how she received her name: "According to a beautiful Chinese legend [Guanyin], when about to enter Heaven, heard a cry of anguish rising from the earth beneath her, and, moved by pity, paused as her feet touched the glorious threshold. Hence her name [which means] one who notices or hears the cry, or prayer, of the world."[51]

Chinese Hell

Besides contributing Guanyin to Chinese mythology, Buddhists also contributed the Chinese version of hell. Many of the major religions, including Christianity and Islam, have a place known as hell, where the souls of evil people go when they die to be punished for their sins. Buddhism brought this concept to China from India, where hell is called *naraka*. In the mythologies of most cultures, hell is a place in which people suffer endlessly; but in Buddhism and some branches of Daoism that also believe in reincarnation of the soul, hell is only a temporary place of punishment. When people die, their souls go to hell, where divine beings judge the good and the bad the people did during their lives. These officials then sentence the souls of the dead for their sins. In her book *Daoism*, mythologist Jennifer Oldstone-Moore explains how Chinese hell operates: "[After] judgment, the soul pays for its crimes by passing through various levels of Hell, where it undergoes torments appropriate to the crimes committed.

At last, the soul reaches the final court where, having atoned for shortcomings in the life just past, it is reincarnated."[52]

As with much of Chinese mythology, there is not much agreement in the myths about hell, which in Chinese is called *diyu*. Various myths describe it with different numbers of courts where people are judged and with hundreds of different areas that feature different types of punishment. Some of the punishments are tailored to the crime: Liars, for example, have their tongues ripped out. Many punishments, however, simply involve excessive heat, excessive cold, sadness, or disease. DuBose writes,

> Every form of torment, mental and physical, that can befall the unhappy violators of a good conscience and of the Buddhist law, are found there [in hell]. The extremes of cold and heat, cutting, flaying, biting, insulting, and tantalizing have to be endured by such persons according to their deserts [the punishment they deserve]. Demons of the most monstrous shapes and most cruel dispositions terrify them in every possible way.[53]

Some hell myths, however, say that people who had been especially good are able to skip punishment for the small number of sins they committed and be reborn immediately.

CHAPTER 5

Chinese Mythology Today

For more than two thousand years, emperors ruled China. For more than two thousand years, belief in mythological tales, divine beings, and fabulous creatures dominated the way the Chinese lived. In their homes people worshipped their ancestors and deities such as Zao Jun and door gods. The Chinese regularly visited religious temples that were decorated with and guarded by statues of dragons, foo dogs, and other mythical beasts. In the temples they made offerings of food and prayed to deities such as the Jade Emperor, Guanyin, and heaven itself. Their daily conversation was sprinkled with pleas for help from the gods and goddesses they worshipped and proverbs connected to the myriad myths that shaped the way they thought and acted.

In the twentieth century the way of life the Chinese had known for two millennia became threatened. On February 12, 1912, the Chinese Revolution (1911–1912) forced Puyi, China's last emperor, to abdicate the throne. His departure ignited more than three decades of civil war that ended on October 1, 1949, when victorious Communists led by Mao Tse-tung established the People's Republic of China (PRC). In their first few decades of rule, the Communists tried to eliminate Chinese religions and banish belief in the myths and tales that until then had played an important role in Chinese life.

The Communists, however, lost that battle, and today ancient religions, traditions, and mythology are still alive in the PRC, as well as in other parts of the world where migrating Chinese have spread them. The Communists failed because the beliefs and cultural practices they were trying to wipe away had been woven so deeply into the hearts and minds of Chinese people for thousands of years that they would not surrender them. The difficulty of that task can be seen in Mao himself. Even though Mao led the attack on such ancient beliefs, he never succeeded in ridding himself of his own ties to them.

Mao Tse-tung

Mao Tse-tung was born on December 26, 1893, in Shaoshan, a village in Hunan Province. Although Mao embraced the harsh life and mentality of China's poverty-stricken peasant class as an adult, he did not grow up poor: His father was a rich farmer and grain merchant. Mao loved his mother, a devoted Buddhist, but he never became religious himself. When she died, Mao praised the compassion and charity she had always shown toward people, even though it was a trait from her Buddhist faith, a religion he would later try to destroy. As the son of a well-off farmer, Mao attended school and studied Confucius and Chinese classics such as *Hsi-yu Chi* (*The Journey to the West*), a book that he would later try to ban.

In 1918 when Mao entered Peking University, he began studying the social and economic theories of German political philosopher Karl Marx, and by 1920 he had become a confirmed believer in communism, an economic system in which the state owns and operates all businesses and there is no private property. The vast majority of China's huge rural population lived in dire poverty and was dominated by royalty and rich farmers, merchants, and businessmen. Mao believed communism was the only way the majority of poor Chinese would ever have better lives. Mao also believed China needed to modernize itself by educating its mostly illiterate population and eliminating its dependency on religion and mythology. One of Mao's prime targets was Confucius, whom he considered a main source of the ancient beliefs that weakened China. Mao explains, "I hated Confucius from the age of eight. [I believed] the emphasis on the honoring of Confucius and the reading of the classics, and advocacy of the old rules of propriety and education and philosophy are part of that semi-feudal culture [that had to be destroyed.] The struggle between the old and new cultures is to the death."[54]

Despite Mao's public hatred of ancient philosophies, he continued to read Chinese classics and sometimes quoted them and Daoist founder Laozi in his writings and speeches. And even though Mao had said he despised Confucius, he once claimed that his book *Quotations from Chairman Mao*, a collection of his own thoughts more commonly known as "The Little Red Book," was comparable to Confucius's Analects. Mao made the comparison because he wanted his own thoughts to be considered as important as those of Confucius, who continued to be respected around the world.

Although he tried to ban mythology and religion in China, Mao sometimes used mythological characters to get people to do what he wanted. In 1966 Mao believed Chinese leaders and officials were straying from Communist doctrine. To get young Communists to oppose them he used the example of Sun Wukong, the Monkey King famed for challenging the authority of other mythological figures, such as the Jade Emperor. In a speech Mao declared, "The local areas must produce several more Sun Wukong to vigorously create a disturbance at the Palace of Heaven [government]."[55] Mao believed the universally known, popular Daoist figure would inspire young people to help him purify Communist ideology.

Millions of young people rallied to Mao's cause in what became known as the Cultural Revolution (1966–1976). For a decade they engulfed China in ideological violence that sought to restore Communist values and strip religion, mythology, and ancient philosophy from Chinese culture.

Monkey King

Sun Wukong, the Monkey King, is one of the most popular Chinese mythical figures. He is featured in many movies, including *Monkey King*, a 2013 movie in which martial arts star Donnie Yen portrays him. There is also an annual festival in fall honoring this heroic but mischievous immortal.

On October 1, 1949, Mao Tse-tung (pictured) proclaimed the founding of the People's Republic of China. Mao tried to eliminate Chinese religions and banish belief in the country's myths and tales.

Temples and artwork featuring deities the Chinese worshipped were destroyed, and millions of people were beaten, tortured, and even killed for holding on to old beliefs.

The Cultural Revolution forced many Chinese to hide their beliefs and quit the traditional practices they had followed for centuries, but when the revolution ended, all the beliefs and traditions had survived. And in the decades that followed, they would once again become an accepted part of Chinese life.

Chinese Religion

Deng Xiaoping became China's leader after Mao died in 1976. In 1978 Deng began instituting policies that moved China toward a more capitalist economic system, one that allowed citizens more personal freedom, including the right to participate in religion. The result was a return by millions of people to religious beliefs based on Chinese mythology.

According to *Spiritual Life Study of Chinese Residents*, a 2007 study conducted by the Chinese polling firm Horizon, 85 percent of Chinese hold religious beliefs or practice some form of religion; this percentage includes 754 million people who participate in various forms of ancestor worship. The study also shows that Buddhism has 185 million followers, the most of any religion, including 12 percent of Communist Party members, even though Communists stress atheism. Although the study said Daoism is believed to have the second largest number of followers, exact numbers are not available. That is because many adherents of Daoism consider it a philosophy and not a religion. Another problem in identifying Daoists is that some of the deities they may worship are also worshipped in other religions. However, in a 2011 article in the journal *Asian Philosophy*, religious researcher Wai Yip Wong claims that folk religion is China's most popular and widespread religion. He writes, "Chinese folk religion is not only a complete religious tradition, but also the most influential and important religious tradition in China. According to [several] studies most of the religious believers in China are actually followers of Chinese folk religion rather than Buddhism or Daoism."[56]

Folk religion was China's first religion. When Buddhism and Daoism began centuries later, they both borrowed beliefs from folk religion, including worshipping ancestors and many deities. The influence folk religion had on the development of Buddhism and Daoism makes it difficult for researchers to document what religion Chinese people practice. For example, followers of all three religions participate in annual festivals for Mazu, a mortal who became a goddess of the sea and is considered a protector of fishermen and sailors.

Mazu's birthday is celebrated annually on Meizhou Island, where myth says she was born in 960. In 2010 on

In 2010 thousands of people flocked to Meizhou Island to celebrate the 1,050th anniversary of Mazu's birth.

the 1,050th anniversary of her birthday, thousands of people flocked to her temple there. One of the Mazu believers was Cheng Zhigui, a member of an opera group who wore a pink-and-white mask and black silk clothes and performed a traditional opera in Mazu's honor. Cheng said, "We perform for Mazu. We believe that she's watching us singing opera. The audience can also watch. But if there are no people here, she'll still be watching us."[57]

Mazu is honored throughout China, and her estimated 160 million followers worship her at more than four thousand temples dedicated to her. Although many temples and religious sites were destroyed in the first few decades of Communist rule, the Mazu temples are among tens of thousands of religious temples that remain in China.

Religious Sites

The most historic and impressive religious site in China is the Temple of Heaven in Beijing, which was built in the fifteenth century. A horseshoe-shaped wall nearly 4 miles (6.4km) long surrounds the huge complex of three main temple areas that include ninety-two buildings. It was here that China's emperors performed annual rites to ask heaven

Chinese Zodiac

Western astrology divides the year into twelve sections, each of them represented by a different sign. For example, people born from July 23 to August 22 are born under the sign of Leo, whose symbol is a lion. People born during each of the twelve sections of the year allegedly have certain personality characteristics, and the section's sign can be used to tell their future. The Chinese have a similar system of twelve animals, called the Chinese zodiac, that explains the general personality traits of the people born in a certain year. For example, for the Chinese, it is prestigious to be born in the year of the dragon because dragons are considered powerful and lucky. It is believed that being born in the year of the dragon will ensure someone will be successful.

Animals of the Chinese zodiac rule for an entire year, rather than just for one-twelfth of the year as with the Western zodiac, starting on the Chinese New Year in a revolving twelve-year cycle. The animals, in order of this cycle, are rat, ox, tiger, rabbit, dragon, snake, horse, goat, monkey, rooster, dog, and pig. The dragon is the only mythological animal in the Chinese zodiac. According to myth, the order of the animals was determined by a great race. The cat and the rat, who were once friends, asked the ox if they could ride on his back, because they were poor swimmers and the race included crossing a river. The cat took a nap and asked the rat to wake it up for the race. But the rat wanted to win the race and never woke up the cat. Thus, the cat failed to become part of the zodiac, and the two became bitter enemies. Just before the finish of the race, the rat jumped off the ox to finish first. The dragon should have easily won, because it can fly. But the dragon, which can produce rain, stopped to end a drought. People around the world enjoy looking up the Chinese zodiac animal that corresponds to the year of their birth.

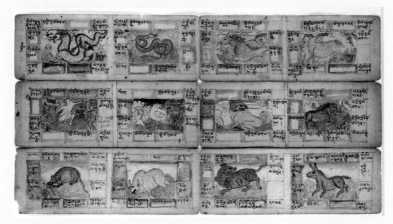

This eighteenth-century Tibetan manuscript depicts the twelve animals in the Chinese zodiac.

for a good harvest, and people sacrificed animals to various gods and ancestors. The Temple of Heaven is decorated in vivid colors of red, gold, green, and blue, and while it does not have the fantastic sculptures of some other temples, it does have ornate carvings on the buildings, including rooftop water drains shaped like the mouths of dragons. The temple architecture itself displays the Chinese belief in the intimate connection between heaven and earth; its design

Chinese Wisdom

A proverb is a saying that expresses a truth based on common sense or practical wisdom derived from the experience of others that has been passed down through generations. Although people from every nation and culture have their own proverbs, the Chinese have always seemed to have more of these wise sayings than other cultures. The reason for China's rich heritage of proverbs is that in traditional Chinese education, students had to memorize selections from ancient texts. One way that people proved they were educated was to use lines from classic books in daily conversation. An example is "There is no way to heaven and there is no gate to hell," which means people will all find their own ways to be either good or bad. According to Hila Berliner, who has researched Chinese sayings, proverbs are still important in the People's Republic of China. In her book Five Flowers Eight Doors: Understanding China and Its Idioms Then and Now, *she explains,*

Proverbs and pearls of wisdom are very much integrated into everyday language in China. People spice up every conversation with folk proverbs and with those borrowed from ancient historians, poets, and philosophers. By presenting philosophical thoughts in a few concise words, the proverbs add color and drama to the everyday spoken language. [The] British philosopher and essayist Francis Bacon (1561–1626) wrote that "The genius, wit and spirit of a nation are discovered in its proverbs." Studying Chinese proverbs is a good way to penetrate deep into Chinese culture. These sayings, passed from generation to generation over more than two thousand years, reflect folk wisdom. Every saying expresses an idea in a concise simple language. Though the sayings are very old, handing them on from generation to generation has molded moral behavior in China. [Some of them] were coined in the folk [and religious] culture and others were borrowed from stories, from philosophers such as Confucius [or] from ancient history books.

Hila Berliner. *Five Flowers Eight Doors: Understanding China and Its Idioms Then and Now*, 2009. www.sin -idioms.blogspot.com.

features contrasting circles, which represent heaven, and squares, which symbolize earth.

The Longxing Temple is located in Hebei Province in Zhengding County. It has towering foo dogs guarding temple entrances as well as colorful representations of various deities, including a 72-foot-tall (22m) statue of Guanyin, the goddess of mercy. The immense figure of one of China's most popular deities has forty-two arms, each of them wielding an object—from the sun and moon to musical instruments.

In Fujian Province eight small villages share a much smaller statue of Guanyin that belongs to the seven-hundred-year-old Chao Tian Temple. Each village keeps the statue for one year. At year's end, villagers hold a feast and carry it on their shoulders back to the Chao Tian Temple. Villagers also carry statues of six other deities so Guanyin will not be lonely on the journey. Wu Jianxian, who lives in Fujian Province, believes the rite shows how important religion is to rural people: "In the cities, people do not have enough belief. I think belief is good, it helps to bring communities together."[58] Such religious festivities are common today in many parts of China. Some annual events involving religion and ancient mythology are even celebrated throughout the entire nation.

Chinese Festivals

The PRC annually celebrates several festivals tied to its past, when the vast majority of its people were farmers in rural areas. The dates of the festivals are calculated using China's ancient lunar calendar, which is based on the movements of the sun and the moon. Dates in the Chinese calendar differ from those in the Western, or Gregorian, calendar, which are calculated by using only Earth's position relative to the sun. For example, the first day of the year in the Gregorian calendar is always January 1, but the first day of the year in the Chinese calendar varies; in 2013 it was February 10 and in 2014 it was January 31. This sounds confusing to Westerners, but Chinese use lunar dates because they are an integral part of ancient traditions celebrated during the festivals.

The most important festival is Chinese Lunar New Year. Also known as the Spring Festival, it is celebrated in China and in Chinese communities throughout the world. The festival begins on Chinese New Year's Eve, which is the last day of the old year, and runs until the fifteenth day of the new year, which is when the first full moon appears. The festival is an important time to honor family and worship dead ancestors. In what is believed to be the world's largest annual mass migration, hundreds of millions of Chinese people travel to their hometowns during this national holiday to reunite with their families. China is such a vast and populous country that New Year travel can be difficult. In 2013 during the Lunar New Year, a record 3.4 billion trips by various means of transportation, including planes, trains, and automobiles were recorded in China.

In the past the New Year was also a time to honor deities and ask for their help in the coming year. The various gods who bestowed wealth and prosperity were among the divine beings people worshipped during this holiday. Some people still pray to various deities, and the standard New Year greeting is "gong xi fa cai," which is Mandarin for "may you prosper." Firecrackers, used in the past to scare away evil spirits, are still an integral part of this holiday, as are dances imitating the movements of lions and dragons. Traditions associated with the New Year include paying off debts and thoroughly cleaning houses on New Year's Eve. However, no cleaning is done after that, because people are afraid they may sweep away the good luck that they might have coming to them in the upcoming year. New Year ends with the Lantern Festival, which was originally a date to honor Taiyi, one of the gods in heaven.

The Hungry Ghost festival is all about ancestor worship. It begins on the fifteenth day of the seventh lunar month when, according to myth, the spirits of the dead are free to roam the world. In an article for *World of Chinese* magazine, Louise Holyoak explains how people celebrate this special period,

New Year Traditions

On the first day of the Lunar New Year, people abstain from eating meat, a sacrifice they make to ensure they will have long and happy lives. People also repay any debts from the previous year and give children "lucky money" in red envelopes to ensure the children's prosperity.

which lasts fourteen days. She writes, "During this festival, which is rooted in Buddhist and Daoist beliefs, Chinese believe that the gates of Hell are opened, releasing hungry ghosts to walk the Earth and seek food. Families celebrate by paying tribute to their dead ancestors, as well as unknown wandering souls, so that they can be put to rest instead of hanging around bringing bad luck to the living."[59]

In addition to offerings of food to honor and appease the dead, people burn fragrant incense and paper money. On the final day of the festival, people float paper lanterns on streams and lakes to help guide the dead back to their resting place.

The Mid-Autumn Festival, held on the fifteenth day of the eighth month of the Chinese calendar, is so culturally important that the PRC made it a national holiday. The festival is associated with giving thanks for the fall harvest and

People in China celebrate the Hungry Ghost Festival, which begins on the fifteenth day of the seventh lunar month and lasts for fourteen days.

worshipping the moon. During the holiday, people eat moon cakes, a round pastry filled with red bean or lotus seed paste. The goddess Chang'e inspired the festival and is still honored during it because myths say she lives on the moon.

Chinese Medicine

Traditional medical practices based on Daoist beliefs from thousands of years ago continue to be used today by the Chinese people. The medical system in the PRC includes all of the modern scientific advances known in the rest of the world. Despite that, traditional Chinese medicine (TCM) is still an important part of Chinese health care. One of the most popular ancient treatments is acupuncture. When a Beijing resident named Lei Dao began suffering from severe pain in his right leg, he tried modern medicine and drugs. Lei did not get relief until he went to Wangjing Hospital in Beijing for acupuncture treatments in which doctors inserted needles into his hip and back. Lei claims he resorted to the ancient practice because "Western medicine can do nothing about my pain and acupuncture works."[60]

Acupuncture is based on Daoist claims that qi (chi), or "life force," travels through everyone's body through channels called meridians and that people become sick because the flow of qi to the body's organs is disrupted or blocked. Medical researcher Ting Hor explains this ancient health theory: "Meridians pass right through the entire body and connect the inner organs to the surface. There are fourteen main ones, with 360 points of contact with the skin from inside the body. By stimulating the meridians, e.g. with needles, qi can be adjusted to re-establish the balance of the body's [life force]."[61]

Centuries ago Daoists mapped out meridians carrying qi and points on the skin in which they could insert tiny needles to stimulate its flow and cure sickness. Scientific studies have been unable to explain what qi is or pinpoint it in the human body. But because acupuncture has been shown to have positive results for a wide variety of medical conditions, it is accepted today throughout the world as a viable alternative to Western medicine. Acupuncturists routinely use needles, some of them heated, to treat people suffering from asthma, arthritis, indigestion, vomiting, headaches, and incontinence. This traditional medical practice is also used to ease pain, depression, and addictions, such as smoking.

TCM includes the use of natural plants and herbs as medicine to treat many illnesses. As with acupuncture, Western doctors were skeptical that plants and herbs used for several thousand years really worked, because there was no scientific data backing up such claims; however, researcher Li Xiu-Min, citing a 2011 U.S. Food and Drug Administration study, concludes, "There is increasing scientific evidence demonstrating that [herbal medicine] has potential for treating asthma and food allergies, and associated conditions."[62] In addition to new scientific evidence that TCM works, Western doctors have

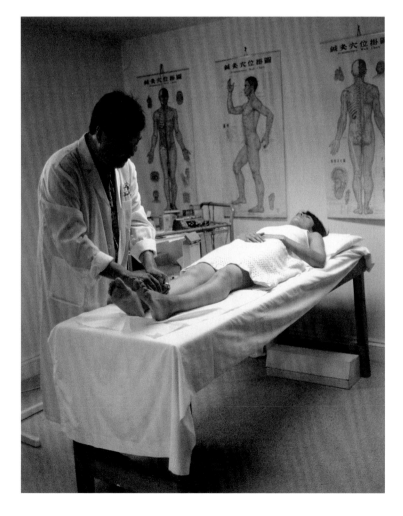

In Chinese medicine one of the most popular ancient treatments is acupuncture.

been increasingly willing to use them because they are often more economical than Western medical practices.

Chinese Culture Goes Global

One ancient Chinese medicine, however, has been accepted more universally than any other: tea. The story of how tea was discovered is yet another Chinese myth. Shennong, a legendary ruler who lived more than five thousand years ago, first brewed tea while testing various herbs and plants for medical purposes. Tea was first used as medicine, but it eventually became a beverage everyone consumed. In the sixteenth century Portuguese and British explorers who went to China took tea back to Europe, where it became a popular beverage. In more recent times Chinese food has also become popular throughout the world. Food and drink, however, are not the only bits of ancient Chinese culture that have spread globally.

Feng shui, which began in China more than three thousand years ago, has also spread around the world. It began

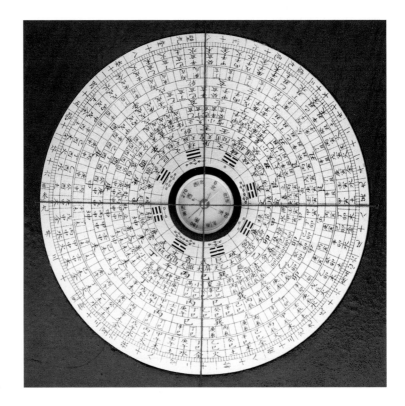

The feng shui compass is used with astrology to tell the future. Feng shui applies Daoist principles such as yin and yang and qi.

as a system of geomancy, a way to tell the future by using a compass and astronomy and applying the readings to Daoist principles, such as yin and yang and qi. Feng shui theory says the earth contains lines of energy that emanate from sleeping dragons, which are believed to live under hills and other higher elevations. This belief led the Chinese to place homes and buildings in spots that would allow inhabitants to benefit from that mystical energy. Feng shui masters, people well versed in feng shui principles, also identify negative spots that people should stay away from. For example, the Chinese believe building a structure on a sleeping dragon, especially on its eyes or head, is unlucky, because it irritates this powerful creature.

Today millions of people throughout the world use feng shui to locate and design buildings and arrange interiors that are beneficial to their lives. In an article for the online magazine *Feng Shui for Modern Living,* Feng shui expert Mark Shackelford writes, "Feng Shui affects every aspect of our life and the way it is applied can be both beneficial and detrimental to the way you live and the surrounding environment. The underlying principle of Feng Shui is to live in harmony with your environment so that the energy surrounding you works for you rather than against you."[63]

Living in harmony with nature is just one of many ancient Daoist principles that have survived to affect how people live today. Chinese martial arts are known today as *wushu* or kung fu. Many styles of *wushu* developed from Daoist physical exercises and Chinese fighting techniques, which also influenced the development of karate, a Japanese martial art. In the second half of the twentieth century, *wushu*'s popularity spawned a new film genre starring Chinese martial artists such as Bruce Lee, Jackie Chan, and Jet Li. Many of those films feature mythical gods and heroes from China's past. In the 2008 martial arts epic *The Forbidden Kingdom*, most of which was shot in China, Chan plays Lu Yun, one of the Eight Immortals, and Li is Sun Wukong, the Monkey King. The movie was a global hit and made more than $125 million. A decade earlier another movie about a Chinese mythological figure made four times that amount. The 1998 animated movie *Mulan* by Walt Disney

Colors in China

In the People's Republic of China, the colors people choose for clothing, decoration, and even works of art often have symbolic importance, extending back to ancient religious beliefs and philosophy. Communist parades during the mid–twentieth century featured red and green color schemes for banners and other decorations, because they are traditional colors. Red is one of the most important colors for the Chinese, because it symbolizes fire, which was once vital to survival because it provided warmth and a means to cook food. During Chinese New Year, red blossoms are everywhere, because the color stands for joy, good luck, and virtue. Green is also an important color for the Chinese, because it symbolizes good health, prosperity, and harmony. Red and green are also important colors in the important Daoist theory of yin and yang, with green symbolizing yin and red yang. Sculptures, pictures, and other works of art from ancient times as well as today often incorporate those colors.

Black is a color that Daoists regard as signifying heaven; that connection has led many people in the past and even today to wear black clothing. While people in the West wear black clothing to mourn a death, the Chinese traditionally wear white to funerals. That is changing today as more Chinese people are wearing black and other somber colors instead of white. Red is never worn to a funeral, because it stands for happiness.

Yellow is also a vital color for the Chinese, because Chinese emperors wore it and because it was used extensively as decoration in Chinese religions. Yellow is considered powerful because it is linked to the earth and because the Chinese believe it helps generate yin and yang. Blue is also a highly regarded color, because it is believed to symbolize immortality, something sought by Daoists and many other ancient Chinese.

Pictures made more than $400 million worldwide. In an article in *Time* magazine, journalist Ling Woo Liu writes that "because of the animated Disney film, the character Mulan has become one of the most recognizable symbols of Chinese culture worldwide."[64]

Even Confucius Is Accepted

Confucius remained a respected philosopher around the world even as the Communists tried to banish him from Chinese culture in the mid-twentieth century. Since then, the Communists' stance on Confucius has changed, and the PRC has even used his prestigious name to boost its global image. Since 2004, China has established more than three hundred Confucius institutes in various countries to promote Chinese language and culture. In 2011 Communist leaders placed a huge statue of Confucius, 31 feet (9.4m) tall and weighing 17 tons (19 tonnes), in the National Museum of China. Lu Zhangshen, curator of the museum, says, "Confucius was seen as a saint by many dynasties in Chinese history. He is the symbol of traditional Chinese culture, with a far-reaching impact across the globe."[65]

The honors bestowed on an ancient sage once reviled by Mao Tse-tung, the architect of Chinese communism, is yet another strong sign of how modern-day China is willing to embrace its ancient past.

Introduction: A Confusing Galaxy of Ancient Myths

1. Quoted in Anne Birrell. *Chinese Mythology: An Introduction*. Baltimore: Johns Hopkins University Press, 1993, p. xi.
2. Quoted in Pierre Grimal, ed. *Larousse World Mythology*. New York: Hamlyn, 1965, p. 10.
3. Endymion Porter Wilkinson. *Chinese History: A Manual*. Rev. ed. Cambridge, MA: Harvard University Asia Center, 2000, p. 567.
4. J.F. Bierlien. *Parallel Myths*. New York: Ballantine, 1994, p. xiii.

Chapter 1: China

5. Quoted in Birrell. *Chinese Mythology*, p. 35.
6. Tsien Tsuen-Hsuin. *Science and Civilisation in China*. Vol. 5, *Chemistry and Chemical Technology*, part 1: "Paper and Printing." Cambridge: Cambridge University Press, 1985, p. 38.
7. Grimal, *Larousse World Mythology*, p. 273.
8. Lihui Yang and Deming An with Jessica Anderson Turner. *Handbook of Chinese Mythology*. Santa Barbara, CA: ABC-CLIO, 2005, p. 4.

9. Quoted in Hampden C. DuBose. *The Dragon, Image, and Demon*. London: S.W. Partridge, 1886. http://ia700202.us.archive.org/15/items/thedragonimage00dubouoft/thedragonimage00dubouoft.pdf.
10. Anthony Christie. *Chinese Mythology*. London: Hamlyn, 1968, p. 24.
11. Kenneth C. Davis. *Don't Know Much About Mythology: Everything You Need to Know About the Greatest Stories in Human History but Never Learned*. New York: HarperCollins, 2005, p. 397.
12. DuBose. *The Dragon, Image, and Demon*.
13. Quoted in Davis. *Don't Know Much About Mythology*, p. 360.

Chapter 2: Creation, Mythical Beasts, and Evil Spirits

14. Christie. *Chinese Mythology*, p. 47.
15. Quoted in William Theodore de Bary et al., comps. *Sources of Chinese Tradition*. Vol. 1. New York: Columbia University Press, 1960, p. 293.
16. Quoted in Samuel Wells Williams. *The Middle Kingdom: A Survey of the Geography, Government, Literature, Social Life, Arts, and History of*

the Chinese Empire and Its Inhabitants. New York: Scribner's, 1913, p. 138.

17. Quoted in DuBose. *The Dragon, Image, and Demon.*

18. Quoted in Te Lin. *Teach Yourself: Chinese Myths.* Chicago: Contemporary Books, 2001, p. 12.

19. Quoted in Birrell. *Chinese Mythology,* p. 33.

20. Anne Birrell. *Chinese Myths.* Austin: University of Texas Press, 2001, p. 20.

21. Quoted in Christie. *Chinese Mythology,* p. 93.

22. Quoted in DuBose. *The Dragon, Image, and Demon.*

23. Quoted in *People's Daily.* "Chinese Dragon Originates from Primitive Agriculture: Archeologist," February 5, 2001. http://english .people.com.cn/english/200102/05 /eng20010205_61559.html.

24. Quoted in *The Classic of Mountains and Seas.* Translated by Anne Birrell. New York: Penguin, 1999, p. 136.

25. Quoted in Jeannie Thomas Parker. *The Mythic Chinese Unicorn,* 2007. http://chinese-unicorn.com/ch01.

26. Quoted in DuBose. *The Dragon, Image, and Demon.*

27. Birrell. *Chinese Mythology,* p. 17.

Chapter 3: Gods and Goddesses

28. E.T.C. Werner. *Myths and Legends of China.* New York: Dover, 1994, p. 93.

29. DuBose. *The Dragon, Image, and Demon.*

30. Mario Poceski. *Introducing Chinese Religions.* New York: Routledge, 2009, p. 169.

31. Jennifer Oldstone-Moore. *Confucianism: Origins, Beliefs, Practices, Holy Texts, Sacred Places.* New York: Oxford University Press, 2002, p. 27.

32. Birrell. *Chinese Mythology,* pp. 40–41.

33. Jonathan Chamberlain. *Chinese Gods: An Introduction to Chinese Folk Religion.* Hong Kong: Blacksmith, 2009, p. 82.

34. Quoted in John Harvey Kellogg. *The Medical Missionary.* Battle Creek, MI: International Medical Missionary and Benevolent Association, 1897, p. 82.

35. Quoted in Daniel Nuckols. "Flood Legends." Creation Science Academy. www.ecreationscience.com /Flood_Legends.html.

36. Birrell. *Chinese Mythology,* p. 160.

37. Quoted in Suzanne E. Cahill. *Transcendence and Divine Passion: The Queen Mother of the West in Medieval China.* Stanford, CA: Stanford University Press, 1993, pp. 12–13.

38. Birrell. *Chinese Mythology,* p. 173.

39. Terhi Mikkolainen. "Mazu: Goddess of the Sea." GBTimes, July 16, 2007. http://gbtimes.com/culture /mazu-goddess-sea.

40. Quoted in Robin R. Wang. *Images of Women in Chinese Thought and Culture: Writings from the Pre-Qin Period Through the Song Dynasty.* Indianapolis, IN: Hackett, 2003, p. 95.

Chapter 4: Confucianism, Daoism, and Buddhism

41. DuBose. *The Dragon, Image, and Demon.*
42. Daniel J. Paracka Jr. "China's Three Teachings and the Relationship of Heaven, Earth and Humanity." *Worldviews: Global Religions, Culture, and Ecology,* vol. 16, no. 1, 2012, p. 76.
43. Jonathan Price. *The Way of Confucius.* London: Compendium, 2010, p. 12.
44. Quoted in DuBose. *The Dragon, Image, and Demon.*
45. Judith A. Berling. "Confucianism." *Focus on Asian Studies,* Fall 1982, p. 7.
46. Robert Eno. "The *Dao de jing.*" Indiana University, Fall 2010. www.indiana.edu/~p374/Daodejing.pdf.
47. Quoted in Joan Chan. "Lao Zi and the Canon of Virtue." *China Eye,* Autumn 2009, p. 12.
48. Quoted in Alasdair Clayre. *The Heart of the Dragon.* New York: Houghton Mifflin, 1985, p. 38.
49. Chan. "Lao Zi and the Canon of Virtue," p. 12.
50. Wu Ch'eng-en. *The Journey to the West.* Vol. 4. Translated and edited by Anthony C. Yu. Chicago: University of Chicago Press, 1983, p. 183.
51. Werner. *Myths and Legends of China,* p. 251.
52. Jennifer Oldstone-Moore. *Daoism: Origins, Beliefs, Practices, Holy Texts, Sacred Places.* London: Watkins, 2011, p. 87.
53. DuBose. *The Dragon, Image, and Demon.*

Chapter 5: Chinese Mythology Today

54. Quoted in John A. Hardon. "Confucianism." In *Religions of the World.* Westminster, MD: Newman Press, 1963. Available at the Real Presence Eucharistic Education and Adoration Society. www.therealpresence.org/archives/Protestantism/Protestantism_025.htm.
55. Quoted in Frederic Wakeman Jr. "The Monkey King." Review of *The Journey to the West.* 2 vols. Translated and edited by Anthony C. Yu. *New York Review of Books,* May 29, 1980. www.nybooks.com/articles/archives/1980/may/29/the-monkey-king/?pagination=false.
56. Wai Yip Wong. "Defining Chinese Folk Religion: A Methodological Interpretation." *Asian Philosophy,* May 2011, p. 153.
57. Quoted in Louisa Lim. "China's Leaders Harness Folk Religion for Their Aims." National Public Radio, July 23, 2010. www.npr.org/2010/07/23/128672542/chinas-leaders-harness-folk-religion-for-their-aims.
58. Quoted in Alison Bailey et al. *China.* New York: DK, 2007, p. 211.
59. Quoted in Louise Holyoak. "How to Celebrate Hungry Ghost Festival." *World of Chinese,* August 16, 2011. www.theworldofchinese.com/2011/08/how-to-celebrate-hungry-ghost-festival.
60. Quoted in Fred Guterl. "Ouch! That Feels Better." *Newsweek,* May 19, 2003, p. 40.

61. Ting Hor. "China: The Full Treatment." *UNESCO Courier,* February 1998, p. 31.

62. Li Xiu-Min. "Treatment of Asthma and Food Allergy with Herbal Interventions from Traditional Chinese Medicine." *Mount Sinai Journal of Medicine,* September-October 2011, p. 712.

63. Mark Shackelford. "How to Use Feng Shui to Improve Your Wealth." *Feng Shui for Modern Living,* Spring 2009. www.fengshui-magazine.com/FSArticle01.pdf.

64. Ling Woo Liu. "China vs. Disney: The Battle for *Mulan.*" *Time,* December 3, 2009. www.time.com/time/world/article/0,8599,1944598,00.html.

65. Quoted in UPI. "Beijing Honors Confucius with Big Statue," January 12, 2011. www.upi.com/Top_News/World-News/2011/01/12/Beijing-honors-Confucius-with-big-statue/UPI-52531294860934.

ancestor worship: Offerings made to the spirits of dead relatives so they will help the living.

Buddhism: A religion founded on the teachings of Siddhartha Gautama, also known as the Buddha.

Confucianism: A code of conduct developed by Confucius that emphasizes obligations of people toward each other and toward their rulers.

Daoism: A religion and philosophy based on the belief in the Dao, or Way.

deity: A god or goddess.

dynasty: A series of rulers of a nation descended from the same family.

folk religion: The earliest religious beliefs that the Chinese developed.

mythologist: A person who is an expert on mythology.

pantheon: All the deities in a given religion.

sacrifice: To offer food and other things to deities.

shaman: A person with magical powers.

spirits: The still-alive souls of people who have died.

the three teachings: The moral philosophies of Confucianism, Daoism, and Buddhism.

yin and yang: Opposing forces such as darkness and light, weakness and strength, death and life, and male and female.

Books

Anne Birrell. *Chinese Mythology: An Introduction*. Baltimore: Johns Hopkins University Press, 1993. This is an excellent book that explains the basic principles underlying Chinese mythology and relates many of its most important myths.

Anne Birrell. *Chinese Myths*. Austin: University of Texas Press, 2001. This is a good source book on Chinese mythology.

Jonathan Chamberlain. *Chinese Gods: An Introduction to Chinese Folk Religion*. Hong Kong: Blacksmith, 2009. This is a good source book on China's first religion, which introduced and shaped early Chinese mythology and culture.

Anthony Christie. *Chinese Mythology*. London: Hamlyn, 1968. This is a fine source on Chinese mythology that includes many interesting pictures, which bring the stories to life.

Alasdair Clayre. *The Heart of the Dragon*. New York: Houghton Mifflin, 1985. This book offers an interesting history of China as well as what the nation is like today.

Kenneth C. Davis. *Don't Know Much About Mythology: Everything You Need to Know About the Greatest Stories in Human History but Never Learned*. New York: HarperCollins, 2005. This book explains how myths are created and how they affect the way people live.

Pierre Grimal, ed. *Larousse World Mythology*. New York: Hamlyn, 1965. This book is an informative look at mythologies from various nations.

Te Lin. *Teach Yourself: Chinese Myths*. Chicago: Contemporary Books, 2001. This book is a solid resource on Chinese mythology.

Jennifer Oldstone-Moore. *Confucianism: Origins, Beliefs, Practices, Holy Texts, Sacred Places*. New York: Oxford University Press, 2002. This book details how the teachings of Confucius came to be a religion and were spread around the world.

Jennifer Oldstone-Moore. *Daoism: Origins, Beliefs, Practices, Holy Texts, Sacred Places*. London: Watkins, 2011. This book provides detailed explanations about Daoism.

Mario Poceski. *Introducing Chinese Religions*. New York: Routledge, 2009. This is a good introduction to Chinese religion.

Jonathan Price. *The Way of Confucius*. London: Compendium, 2010. This is a fine biography that explains Confucius's teachings and how they affected China and other parts of the world.

Jeremy Roberts. *Chinese Mythology A to Z*. 2nd ed. New York: Chelsea House, 2010. Written in alphabetical order like a dictionary, this book details various myths and deities. It is available for free at www.cs.rutgers .edu/~mcgrew/remusleftovers/ipad /chinesemythology.pdf.

E.T.C. Werner. *Myths and Legends of China*. New York: Dover, 1994. This book, written by a twentieth-century British diplomat to China, provides an invaluable look at how the Chinese perceived mythology before the Communists won political control of China. It is available for free at www .sacred-texts.com/cfu/mlc/mlc00.htm.

Lihui Yang. *Handbook of Chinese Mythology*. Santa Barbara, CA: ABC-CLIO, 2005. This book is an excellent source on Chinese myths.

Internet Sources

Birgitta Augustin. "Daoism and Daoist Art." Metropolitan Museum of Art. www.metmuseum.org/toah/hd/daoi /hd_daoi.htm. This article explains Daoism in Chinese art and includes images.

Hampden C. DuBose. *The Dragon, Image, and Demon*. London: S.W. Partridge, 1886. http://ia700202. us.archive.org/15/items/thedragon image00dubouoft/thedragonimage 00dubouoft.pdf. This book, written by a nineteenth-century Christian missionary, explains ancient Chinese myths and culture.

Websites

Cultural China (www.cultural-china .com). This is a nonprofit website dedicated to promoting the Chinese culture around the world. It is a good source of information on Chinese traditions, arts, history, and cultural news.

Encyclopedia Mythica (www.pantheon .org). This website is an encyclopedia of mythology, folklore, and religion. Select "Chinese" in the "Jump to Area" box for brief information on individual figures in Chinese mythology.

Internet Encyclopedia of Philosophy (www.iep.utm.edu). This website provides information in all areas of philosophy, including good explanations of various Chinese philosophies, such as Confucianism and Daoism.

Living in the Chinese Cosmos (http:// afe.easia.columbia.edu/cosmos/bgov /intro.htm). Offered by Columbia University, this website is an excellent source of information about Chinese religions.

Mythology Dictionary (www.mytholo gydictionary.com). This website is an online dictionary of terms pertaining to myths around the world. Enter "Chinese" in the search box for a list of Chinese gods, heroes, and other mythological characters.

Society for Anglo-Chinese Understanding (www.sacu.org). This is the website for the Society for Anglo-Chinese Understanding, a charity in the United Kingdom that promotes friendship and understanding between Britain and China. The site offers many excellent articles on Chinese history, language, geography, and culture.

INDEX

PICTURE CREDITS

Cover: © Nicha/Shutterstock.com

© AFP/Getty Images, 78

© Annabella Bluesky/AcuMedic/Science Source, 87

© Argus Photo/Alamy, 88

© Beaconstox/Alamy, 55

© BnF, Dist. RMN-Grand Palais/Art Resource, NY, 37

© British Library Board/Robana/Art Resource, NY, 14

© Cengage Learning, 4, 5

The Demons of Blackwater River Carry Away the Master, illustration from 'Myths and Legends of China', by Edward T.C. Werner, pub. by George G. Harrap & Co., 1922 (colour litho), English School, (20th century)/Private Collection/The Bridgeman Art Library, 41

Feeding Silkworms and Sorting Cocoons, engraved by A. Willmore (engraving), Allom, Thomas (1804-72) (after)/Private Collection/The Stapleton Collection/The Bridgeman Art Library, 33

A figure of Guandi seated, 14th-15th century (carved ivory), Chinese School/Private Collection/Photo © Heini Schneebeli/The Bridgeman Art Library, 50

© GL Archive/Alamy, 20

Heng O Flies to the Moon, illustration from 'Myths and Legends of China', by Edward T.C. Werner, pub. by George G. Harrap & Co., 1922 (colour litho), English School, (20th century)/Private Collection/The Bridgeman Art Library, 57

© Iain Masterton/Alamy, 36

Lao-Tzu (c.604–531) on his buffalo, followed by a disciple (w/c on paper), Chinese School, (18th century)/Bibliotheque Nationale, Paris, France/Archives Charmet/The Bridgeman Art Library, 67

© Lin Jianbing/Xinhua/Landov, 80

© Lordprice Collection/Alamy, 11

© Melvyn Longhurst/SuperStock, 72

© Mengzhzng/Dreamstime.com, 31

The Monkey King Sun Wukong, Edo period, 1812 (colour woodblock print), Shumman, Kubo (1757–1820)/Arthur M. Sackler Gallery, Smithsonian Institution, USA/The Anne van Biema Collection/The Bridgeman Art Library, 71

© nagelesstock.com/Alamy, 24

© Olaf Schubert/Imagebroker/Alamy, 69

Pangu (engraving), English School, (18th century)/Private Collection/The Bridgeman Art Library, 8

© Peter Horree/Alamy, 29, 61

© Tang Xianjiang/Xinhua/Landov, 85

© TAO Images Limited/Alamy, 23

The Taoist Court of Infernal Justice (gouache on paper), Chinese School, (20th century)/Private Collection/Archives Charmet/The Bridgeman Art Library, 44

© The Trustees of the British Museum/Art Resource, NY, 62

© Universal History Archive/Getty Images, 49, 81

© Victor Paul Borg/Alamy, 52

ABOUT THE AUTHOR

Michael V. Uschan is the author of more than ninety books, including *Life of an American Soldier in Iraq*, for which he won the 2005 Council for Wisconsin Writers Juvenile Nonfiction Award. It was the second time he won the award. Uschan began his career as a writer and editor with United Press International, a wire service that provided stories to newspapers, radio, and television, and he considers writing history books a natural extension of the skills he developed in his many years as a journalist. Uschan and his wife, Barbara, reside in the Milwaukee suburb of Franklin, Wisconsin.